Leonard Manasseh & Partners

Twentieth Century Architects

THE
TWENTIETH
CENTURY
SOCIETY

ENGLISH HERITAGE

RIBA ⊞ Publishing

Leonard Manasseh & Partners

Twentieth Century Architects

Timothy Brittain-Catlin

Published by RIBA Publishing, 15 Bonhill Street, London
EC2P 2EA

ISBN 978 1 85946 368 0

Stock Code 73088

British Library Cataloguing-in-Publication Data
A catalogue record for this book is available from the
British Library.

Publisher: Steven Cross
Commissioning Editor: Lucy Harbor
Series Editors: Barnabas Calder, Elain Harwood and Alan
Powers
Project Editor: Susan George
Copy Editor: Ian McDonald
Typeset by Carnegie Book Production
Printed and bound by The Charlesworth Group, Wakefield

RIBA Publishing is part of RIBA Enterprises Ltd.
www.ribaenterprises.com

Front cover photo: The National Motor Museum, Beaulieu
Photo © English Heritage – James O. Davies

Back cover photo: Leonard Manasseh, left, with Ian Baker,
and Zac Manasseh's model of the National Motor Museum
Photo by Derek Balmer

Frontispiece photo: The entrance court at Rutherford
School, Marylebone, London, with Leonard Manasseh's
sculptures in the foreground

Foreword   vii
Acknowledgements   viii
Introduction   xiii

1 Foundations   1
2 Parterre   13
3 Piano Nobile   53
4 Loggia   87
5 Cornice   119
6 Skyline   135

List of Works   139
Bibliography   155
Index   157
Picture Credits   162

Foreword

It is interesting to see the work of practices such as Leonard Manasseh's represented in a time that no longer knows the practices' context, beliefs and sense of destiny. All significant architecture must go through this process, where its originating thought and circumstances fall away and it becomes an object upon which successive generations project their own views. In the perspective of the present what can be learned from the work of Leonard Manasseh's practice flows from its combination of form making and social content. What distinguished it from its more canonically modernist peers in post-war Britain was the freedom with which imagery and technique from tradition were incorporated with vigorous modernism. Like H.T. Cadbury-Brown at the Royal College of Art or Chamberlin Powell and Bon in Golden Lane and the Barbican, or for that matter Stirling and Gowan, there was an understanding that architecture did not come just from analysis, but also from interpretation of its existential and cultural background. In Leonard Manasseh's work this translated into the designing of beautiful forms, both as a creative activity within architecture and as a gift to the broader public. As architecture the Rutherford School, with a roofline composed of a pyramid and an equal but inverted form, has enjoyed constant quiet admiration from several generations of the profession and was part of the mental world in which I designed the Lisson Gallery. As a public offering, the confident placing of the building in its very different surroundings and the feeling for occupation that gave it an interior miraculously containing Carrara marble and a courtyard of abstract sculptural objects has led to its being a building loved by its users.

TONY FRETTON

opposite **The National Motor Museum: looking towards the entrance from the cycle gallery.**

Acknowledgements

I am indebted to many people who freely gave of their time to help put this book together. First of all I would like to thank the Manasseh family — Leonard, of course, but especially Phin, Sarah, Zac, Sylvia, Amos, Di and Jill, Roseann Rea, David Rea, my mother Jennifer Balfour of Burleigh, and brother Daniel Brittain-Catlin — for their invaluable help throughout. I also spent some time with the late Ian Baker, and Nina Baker has generously read and commented on drafts, and researched her father's archive. I am very grateful to Robert Carsen, and Cosmo and Francis Fry, for their generous help with the section relating to Jeremy Fry, and to Hon. Ralph Montagu and Kenneth Robinson CBE for reading and commenting on the references to Beaulieu. Edward Bottoms, archivist at the Architectural Association, kindly answered a large number of questions for me, and also helped with illustrations.

For all the descriptions of working life in the office and many other details I would like to thank Annabel Ayres, Susan Bell, Alex Billeter, John Birkett-Smith, Lord Cunliffe, David Etherton, Valerie de Fontanals, Nigel Honer, Sir Michael Hopkins, Robert Huddleston, Donald Meyer, Roger W. Morgan, Richard Partridge, Stuart Ross, John Thake, Muriel Webb and Nigel Woolner; and, for descriptions of Leonard Manasseh's time at the AA, Tony Fretton, Peter Ahrends, Paul Koralek and Elia Zenghelis. For help with descriptions and documentation of the partnership's projects, I would like to thank Lord Montagu of Beaulieu and his staff — especially Jackie Bethel, Doug Hill and Margaret Rawles. I also acknowledge the kind help of Hugh Alexander, National Archives; Nicky Arthur, Bristol City Council; Mr and Mrs Philip Bailey; Peter Bale and Barbara Wright (Estates Department), and Alex Cave (Archives), University of Leicester; Dr Derek Balmer PPRWA; Neil Bingham and Mark Pomeroy, Royal Academy of Arts; Tim Borrett, Teignbridge District Council; Dr Nicholas Bullock; Michael Carden; Tony Chapman; Pamela Clark and Alison Derrett, Royal Archives; Professor Mark Connelly; Freddie Cottis, Peter Eaton and Ken Simms; John Crowther; John Curtis; Alison Dalby, Robert Gray and Judith Plante Cleall, National Trust; Janet Dobbins and Lee Harris, North Dorset District Council; David Devine, Museum of Harlow; Martin Dover; Peter France and Alastair Spurr, Rotork plc; Andy Foyle; Nic Fulcher, Leeds Castle; Andy Garnett; Matt Gibberd; Joe Hayward; Kate Head and Lauren Walker, Royal Library Windsor; Chris Higgs, Aggregate Industries; Kate Irvine; Mike Kelly; Geoff King and Alan McLaughlin, Centrica; Janet King; John Kress, James Cubitt & Partners; Peter Lewis, Hordle Walhampton School; Alet Mans, Hopkins Architects Ltd; Belinda Marking, Aberystwyth University; Elspeth Millar, British Library Sound Archive; Michelle Moore, University of Loughborough; Elizabeth Morrissey, King Solomon Academy; Susan Patterson, Royal Bank of Scotland Group plc; Nicholas Ray; Anita Ronke, Aspers Group Ltd; Penny Russell, Windsor Castle Education Centre; Peter Sapsed; Jennifer Singer; Moira Smith, Bolton Abbey; David Sugden; Sarah Thomas, Furzedown Halls of Residence; Philip Uren; Tracy Wilkinson, Archive Centre, King's College, Cambridge; and the staff of the RIBA Library and the London Metropolitan Archives.

For vital help with illustrations, I would like to thank Rupert Thomas, who does so much for architectural history; Brett Croft, Eleanor Sharman and Maria Yiannikkou at Condé Nast; Sophie Burton, June Warrington and Emma Whinton-Brown and their colleagues, National Monuments Record Centre; Stephen Setford, Phineas Manasseh; Louise Oliver, Royal Collection; Miranda Jacobs and Louise Holt, Royal West of England Academy; Catherine Slessor, *Architectural Review*; Valerie Bennett, AA Photo Library; and, at the University of Kent, Howard Griffin, Brian Wood, Dele Ojo and Pier-Luigi del Renzio, of the Kent School of Architecture; and Derek Whittaker, Templeman Library.

My thanks of course to Elain Harwood and Alan Powers for their promotion and support of this project as well as much help with my research, and particularly to Barnabas Calder for his work on the text; to James O. Davies; to Professor Don Gray, Head of the Kent School of Architecture, University of Kent, for allowing me the time to write the book; and to my commissioning editor Lucy Harbor and project editor Susan George at RIBA Publishing.

The research for and production of this book were generously supported by the family of the late Ian Baker; William Brittain-Catlin; The John S. Cohen Foundation; Lord and Lady Cunliffe; Sir Michael and Lady Hopkins; Amos Manasseh; Rotork plc; Sir John and Lady Sorrell; Nigel and Carol Woolner; and the University of Kent, which granted the author study leave in which to write it during the Spring term of 2010.

THE TWENTIETH CENTURY SOCIETY

Without the Twentieth Century Society an entire chapter of Britain's recent history was to have been lost. It was alert when others slept. It is still crucial!

Simon Jenkins, writer, historian, journalist

Love it or hate it, the architecture of the twentieth century has shaped our world: bold, controversial, and often experimental buildings that range from the playful Deco of seaside villas to the Brutalist concrete of London's Hayward Gallery.

Arguably the most vibrant, dynamic and expressive period of architecture in history, the twentieth century generated a huge range of styles. You don't have to love them all to believe that the best of these exciting buildings deserve to be protected, just like the masterpieces of the Victorian era that many likewise once thought to be eyesores. Buildings that form the fabric of our everyday life — office blocks, schools, flats, telephone boxes, department stores — are often poorly understood.

The campaign to protect the best of architecture and design in Britain from 1914 onwards is at the heart of the Twentieth Century Society. Our staff propose buildings for listing, advise on restoration and help to find new uses for buildings threatened with demolition. Tragedies like the recent demolition of Modernist House Greenside, however, show how important it is to add your voice to the campaign.

Join the Twentieth Century Society, and not only will you help to protect these modern treasures, you will also gain an unrivalled insight into the groundbreaking architecture and design that helped to shape the century.

www.c20society.org.uk

opposite The finished goods and packing area at Rotork, near Bath, photographed by Colin Westwood in 1968.

Introduction

Leonard Manasseh & Partners were architects' architects; they were not well known to the public but they were widely admired by their peers, their work featuring regularly in professional publications and exhibitions. Leonard Manasseh, who founded the practice after winning a prestigious Festival of Britain competition in 1950, has himself remained a popular and prominent member of every organisation he belongs to. He was admired, even idolised, as a teacher at the Architectural Association and was its President during one of its stormiest periods. He was elected a Royal Academician, and was active too in the Royal Institute of British Architects and the Royal West of England Academy. The buildings designed by the partnership – by himself, by his partner Ian Baker, or under the partners' close guidance – have a distinct and recognisable style which is both of its era and also quite unlike the work of contemporaries, Manasseh putting his personal stamp on work that drew inspiration from Le Corbusier, from Italy and from Scandinavia.

The partnership's work is important, too, because in addition to much else it expresses one of the central themes of 1950s and 1960s architecture: the apparent conflict between the idea of the architect as the creative artist on the one hand, and as the rational technologist and scientist on the other. Manasseh believed that the architect should bring both sides together in a building that resolves the aspirations of its owners without compromising either on its aesthetics or on its construction. In the view of Nigel Honer, who joined the practice from Powell & Moya in the mid-1970s, Manasseh's work had a 'searing intellectual honesty', defining a hugely artistic creative standard of a kind that has since disappeared almost entirely from the architectural profession.

Manasseh's own aspirations were magnificently realised by two remarkable clients who were, like him, equally at home in the world of engineering and the arts and who were passionate about both: Jeremy Fry, for whom he built the Rotork works in Bath; and Lord Montagu of Beaulieu, the founder and moving force behind the National Motor Museum at Beaulieu in Hampshire. This latter project, one of the most far-sighted of any venture of its kind undertaken by a private landowner, turned out also to mark a watershed in modern planning history: it was here that the partnership's consultant Elizabeth Chesterton demonstrated how a visionary private concept could play an important role in the modern, centralised and democratic public planning process. Thus, in a sense, Manasseh prolonged the best of the values of the Festival of Britain, as well as its colour and its fun, for a further 40 years, and it is hardly surprising that almost everyone who worked for the partnership remembers their time there as one of the happiest of their lives.

opposite The porch canopy of the National Motor Museum.

1   Foundations

At the beginning of the 20th century, the Manasseh family were Sephardi merchants of Mesopotamian origin who were brokers in jute and other commodities in the Far East. Saleh Manasseh – tall, fair, blue-eyed, 'a man of intelligence and learning' – left Baghdad in 1862, and, after marrying Esther Cohen – by contrast a 'tiny, fierce, strong' woman from the Iraqi community of Calcutta – established the firm of S. Manasseh & Co. both there and in Singapore.[1] Saleh Manasseh died young, but six of his many sons continued the family business: two in Calcutta, two in Singapore, and, eventually, two in London. The firm had been established to profit from the opium trade that thrived in the eastern outposts of the British Empire; the move to rubber and jute, mainly for the making of gunny bags, occurred when the drug became illegal. Business thrived well enough for Ezekiel, Saleh's second son who ran the Singapore branch, to build himself a mansion, Eden Hall, in the Tanglin district, in 1903.[2]

Ezekiel's partner in Singapore was his younger brother Rupert, but Rupert married a Belgian woman who preferred to live in Brussels. This brought another brother, Alan, over from Calcutta to help manage the business. Soon after arriving in Singapore Alan married Esther Elias, the sister of Joseph Elias, a tin and rubber merchant, newspaper proprietor and property developer who was one of the colony's most prosperous residents, and who supported all his brothers and sisters, as well as nephews and nieces, in houses he had built for them around Amber Road.[3] Esther's father, who like Alan's had died young, was also of Baghdadi origin, but her mother's family was more mixed. The Manasseh and Elias families, like all traders in the British-ruled areas of the East, spoke English to each other, but Esther also spoke Spanish, Arabic, and enough Malay to address the servants; her maternal grandfather had been Ashkenazi, from Austria, and her maternal grandmother may have been a Creole. In addition there were Salonikan or Turkish origins to both her family and Esther Cohen's. On marrying, Alan and Esther moved into Ezekiel's house, and Leonard Saleh Manasseh, their first child, was born there on 21 May 1916. Two years later Sylvia was born; and, after an interval of eight years, there followed a second daughter, Gladys Estelle, always called Gem.

Although Leonard Manasseh later changed his middle name to Sulla, like the Roman general, he remained proud of his origins: Tony Fretton remembers hearing his retort to Cedric Price during a debate at the Architectural Association (AA) in the 1960s when Price said that they had long been on Christian-name terms: 'I don't have a Christian name', said Manasseh. Certainly his childhood, although odd by modern standards, was not all that unusual for the children of the Jewish merchants of the East. He was sent to preparatory school in England, Fernden near Haslemere in Surrey,

opposite **A military airfield scene by Leonard Manasseh, October 1945 (detail).**

above top **Eden Hall in Singapore, birthplace of Leonard Manasseh.**
above left **Sylvia and Leonard Manasseh in the early 1920s.**
above right **Leonard Manasseh in Portugal, 1939.**

and from there to Cheltenham College in Gloucestershire, supported by Joseph Elias because the depression of the late 1920s had hit the Manasseh firm. During school holidays, he and his sister Sylvia stayed with a naval widow in Havant who took in 'Empire children'. After that, the two of them were dispatched to the house near Oxford of David Elias, an uncle by marriage, who ruled over them dictatorially with the help of a group of amahs from Singapore. Together with the Elias' eight children, Leonard and Sylvia slept in boys' and girls' dormitories. During the whole of his education he saw his father only once in 25 years, for three weeks after leaving Cheltenham when he travelled to Calcutta, whither Alan had been obliged to return following the illness and absence in England of his oldest brother Maurice.

The delicious, wonderful AA

Manasseh's first ambition was to be an aircraft pilot, but his father prohibited it. His next idea was to be a journalist, but he seems to have considered himself too lazy to take it up as a profession. His mother thought he ought to be an architect, but Manasseh was so bad at mathematics that he thought that impossible too. He had, however, always been an enthusiastic artist and Cheltenham had encouraged him. After completing his School Certificate in 1934 and his trip to Calcutta, he spent a term at an art school: since Manasseh remembers Mark Gertler being a teacher there, it may have been the Westminster School of Art in Vincent Square. This put him, he later said, on 'the very last hem on the fringe of the Bloomsbury Group', an auspicious start for an architect who was to teach and practise nearly all his life in the immediate vicinity of Bedford Square.[4] From here, he was persuaded by his mother to try architecture school and he chose the AA for the reason that it did not require any proficiency at mathematics.

Manasseh arrived at the school in 1935, initially at the prep studio (as the foundation unit was then called) where he was taught by Robert Furneaux Jordan. Almost everything that subsequently shaped his career, and his circle of friends, grew from his time at the school.[5] He was not an especially strong student, at least at first. Nevertheless, as he later said, he immediately 'loved every minute' of the 'delicious, wonderful AA'.[6] It was a welcome contrast to the oppressive household in Oxford, which he left at 5.00 a.m. every morning and to which he still had to return every night: his tyrannical uncle insisted on him obtaining the signature of the school porter if he left the school late in the evening, to ensure that he had not been lying about where he was spending his evenings. It seems to have been Manasseh's passion for the school that awakened his real interest in architecture. The first of the lifelong friends that he made there was a student in his year, Susan Babington Smith. Through her he got to know her eventual husband Anthony Cox, one of the group of students from the year above who in 1938 rebelled against an attempt to make the AA's regime more conservative. He met James Cubitt, who was in his own year from the start, and the Hungarian-born refugee Stefan Buzás, who joined his unit in 1939. That year, he also met Philip Powell. All these and

their families became enduring friends. His most conspicuous success of the time came in March 1937 when he won a student prize for the design of a school, in a competition organised by the *News Chronicle* newspaper.[7] He spent the summer of 1939 on holiday in Portugal with an AA friend, Eric Brown, and managed to return to England only with some difficulty after war broke out. With Buzás and other friends, he rejoined the evacuated AA at Mount House, Hadley Common in Hertfordshire, an escape at last from Oxford; he shared a neo-Palladian house called Fairholt, in Hadley Green Road, and threw himself into the school's many fondly remembered social events, performing in its pantomimes and plays. In 1940, for example, he performed a solo sketch in *Midnight Mania* entitled 'Balderdash and Bunkum'.

Manasseh's connection with the school never ended; it was interrupted only by his military service and a short stay back in Singapore in the early 1950s. For two years, following his graduation in 1941, he was involved with war work at Command Royal Engineers in North London, and then as assistant architect with Guy Morgan & Partners; during all that time, he was also teaching at the AA and at the Kingston School of Art under Brown. He was then called up into the Fleet Air Arm; finally ignoring his father's prohibition, he trained as a pilot in Canada and then acted as an instructor in Scotland. Here he crashed an aeroplane into the sea, ending further flying.

above **Leonard Manasseh (left) in Portugal, 1939.**

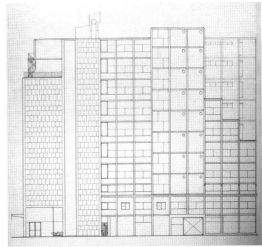

In 1946, he spent his demobilisation payment on a trip to Denmark and Sweden, visiting work by Erik Gunnar Asplund whose Woodland Cemetery in Stockholm left a deep impression. The Scandinavian countries, where modern architecture had continued to develop during the war and housing standards had been transformed in a relatively short period of time, were, he thought, the 'civilised' ones.[8] After returning to England and starting to work, he continued to do some teaching at the AA – eventually becoming a member of staff from 1951 until 1959. During this time, he built up a new set of relationships with students and, to a lesser extent perhaps, the other staff; the Smithsons were 'very clever', he later said, probably not intending to convey much warmth.[9] Peter Ahrends, Richard Burton and Paul Koralek entered the AA in September 1951 (first project: 'Primitive Hut'). Ahrends and Koralek remember clearly how much Manasseh, who together with Ian Baker and Olive Sullivan taught them in their first year, cared about his students, and how much he involved them in his own tremendous optimism. He saw architecture as a part of life, as a way of making life better, rather than something that had a proclamatory quality of its own; he arranged events such as picnics, and a day on which students were bussed off to his own house to do some building work in it. For Ahrends, who had only weeks before 'fled' (as he put it)

above left Stefan Buzás (centre) with Leonard Manasseh, late 1939.
above right Leonard Manasseh's student work at the AA.

racially segregated South Africa, Manasseh seemed to personify everything that he had hoped to find in England.[10]

It was perhaps unfortunate that Manasseh was elected President of the AA in 1964, for a one-year term of office, because it coincided with the climax of one of the most bitter disputes at the school in recent times. Alternatively, perhaps it was a blessing because Manasseh was a calming influence and a diplomatic negotiator in every organisation in which he was involved. The point in question was the proposed merger between the AA and Imperial College, part of the University of London. The President and most of the presiding Council and staff were in favour because the deal offered a move to new and better-equipped premises in South Kensington, and because teachers would acquire the job security enjoyed by university lecturers. In addition, the staff believed that architecture students would profit from proximity to scientists and from a broader educational context – a point made by Manasseh himself on more than one occasion, in particular as a major theme in his presidential address of 1964. Most students and the more radical staff, however, opposed the deal, in part for sentimental reasons but also precisely because they thought that tenure for teachers would deprive the school of its cutting edge. Throughout Manasseh's period in office, the AA's journal, *Arena*, was filled with angry correspondence, mainly favourable to those who wanted to

opposite above A military airfield scene by Leonard Manasseh, October 1945.
opposite below A wartime composition October 1945, Leonard Manasseh's characteristic elongated, happy figures are already evident.
above Leonard Manasseh in the Fleet Air Arm, c.1943.

retain independence. This prolonged affair, in which the students eventually triumphed, does not appear to have dimmed the affection of its participants for the President, who arrived at an AA party when the merger crisis was at its peak dressed as a Roman emperor in a pink toga.[11] Students of nearly 40 years later remember with affection his continuing appearances at school events.[12]

The breakthrough

In 1946, following his Scandinavian tour and during a period of communal living in London, Manasseh took up the position of Assistant Architect at the newly established Architect's Department of Hertfordshire County Council. Under its County Architect C. H. Aslin, Hertfordshire was the right place to be for an optimistic architect who wanted to make modern architecture part of a civilised life. Anthony Cox and other AA friends, most notably David Medd, arrived at Hertford at much the same time to work on projects for the school-building group under Stirrat Johnson-Marshall. The county had few architectural responsibilities beyond the work of its Education Department,

above **Leonard Manasseh in the early 1960s.**

however, and Manasseh designed police stations, and standard houses of a typically Swedish type.[13] In October 1947, he married the textile designer Karin Williger, a friend of Buzás whom he had met when visiting her brother while on army service in Scotland. The following year they moved to Datchworth, north of Welwyn, so that Manasseh could take up the position of Senior Architect under Clifford Holliday at the newly established Stevenage New Town Corporation.[14]

In this job, Manasseh designed a block of maisonettes above shops that still stands at the corner of Popple Way and Sish Lane, at the centre of the first part of the town to be developed. He also drew up an early version of the plan for the town's central pedestrian precinct that was eventually adopted, following considerable opposition by retailers, in 1954. However, the atmosphere was uncongenial and Manasseh feared that he was about to be sacked. Perhaps for this reason he entered, towards the end of 1949, one of only two architectural competitions for structures for the Festival of Britain, that for a luxury restaurant. He did the work for the project from his cottage in Datchworth, producing the drawings as his sister Sylvia, by now a sculptor, typed up the specification late into the evening of 6 November for the deadline the following day. Early the following morning, Manasseh drove up to London to deliver the scheme – almost crashing the car with exhaustion.[15]

above **The Festival restaurant competition perspective, 1949.**

There were 67 entries to the competition: when the results were announced on 11 January 1950 Manasseh's scheme was placed first, ahead of Patrick Gwynne's. The restaurant took the form of a series of standard industrial barrel-vaulted 'Dutch barns' – that is, simple steel sheds – with a 9.14 metre (30 foot) span, forming an L-shape overall and clad with colourful panels of glass, perspex, render and corrugated asbestos sheeting. The building was to be decorated with flags, pennants, and bold numerals spelling out '1951'. The restaurant itself was on the upper floor, entirely glazed towards the river on the south side, and below it were a large entry hall and kitchens, cloakrooms and lavatories. A cantilevered terrace with a crystal dance floor projected over the river. In their report, the assessors – who included Robert Furneaux Jordan, Misha Black and Hugh Casson – praised the 'ingenious and economic' use of the barns, and the 'air of luxury, gaiety and elegance' promised by the scheme.[16] It was the only professional architectural competition that he was ever to win. The pleasure of success was doubled for Manasseh because his friends Philip Powell and Hidalgo Moya won the Festival's other competition, for a 'vertical feature', with what became the Skylon.

Winning the competition promised to provide Manasseh with the opportunity to establish his own office, as Powell and Moya had already done in 1946. The funding to establish the office was put up by Manasseh's Singapore uncle, Joseph Elias; Manasseh's sister Sylvia remembers helping out, too, by paying the rent in the early days when projects were scarce. He gave in his notice and started to work on the restaurant scheme. However, after a few months Herbert Morrison, Lord President of the Council and the minister in charge of the Festival, faced with one of the country's recurrent currency crises and under pressure to reduce costs further, decided to scrap the restaurant. Manasseh was informed that the project was cancelled.[17]

Notes

1   Saleh Manasseh: quoted from a contemporary without further attribution in Eze Nathan, *The Jews of Singapore (1830–1945)*, Singapore, Herbilu, 1986, p6. This description of Manasseh's early life is derived from the author's conversations with Sylvia Manasseh (2 March 2010); Roseann Rea (4 and 14 March 2010); Jennifer, Lady Balfour of Burleigh (4 March 2010, etc.); Leonard Manasseh interviewed by Louise Brodie, 1998, 'Architects' Lives', British Library Sound Archive, reference C467/27 [Manasseh BL interviews], especially Tape 1, Tape 2 Side A; and the author's own family knowledge.

2   The house was designed by Swan & Maclaren who also built business premises for the firm, and who had been the architects for the Teutonia Club which the brothers bought and turned into the Goodwood Park Hotel. Eden Hall, which still stands, was for a long time the residence of the British High Commissioner, and still has its flagpole. Interestingly, Regent Alfred John Bidwell, the architect at Swan & Maclaren who designed the house, was an AA graduate originally from Wimbledon, elected a member in 1886.

3   Elias is generally credited with building Singapore's first block of flats, Amber Mansions, which also housed various members of his family.

4   Manasseh BL interviews, Tape 1 Side A.

5   Student attendance records: Architectural Association Archives, A502. The author's thanks to Edward Bottoms for a great deal of help on this section.

6   Manasseh BL interviews, Tape 2 Side A, Tape 1 Side B.

7   The competition was between students from the AA, Bristol and Liverpool schools, following the one for professionals won in March 1937 by Denis Clarke Hall.

8   Manasseh reiterated this at his talk at the Royal Academy, London, on 24 November 2006.

9   In a conversation with the author in October 2006.

The Smithsons, together with Theo Crosby and Ronald Simpson, had submitted an unplaced design for the Festival restaurant (see below).

10 Author's conversation with Peter Ahrends and Paul Koralek, 26 February 2010.

11 Fondly remembered by Nigel Woolner, 12 March 2010.

12 Jennifer Singer, a graduating student in 2001, told this author for example that Manasseh had joined a student trip that year to the Eden Centre (designed by Nicholas Grimshaw, an opponent of the merger).

13 Houses include 'Type A', dated 20 September 1946. They were probably intended for police officers since the county council did not have general housing responsibilities.

14 For Karin Manasseh, see her biographical and autobiographical notes, 'Karin's Story',
in a contribution to Geoffrey Rayner, Richard Chamberlain, Annamarie Stapleton, eds, *Jacqueline Groag*, Woodbridge, ACC Editions, 2009, pp13–17, which includes her drawing of Susan Cox, her flatmate before Anthony Cox's demobilisation. Karin's brother, Thomas Weiss, worked at the Camphill-Rudolf Steiner School near Aberdeen; further reference in Manasseh BL interviews, Tape 3 Side B.

15 Conversation with Sylvia Manasseh, 2 March 2010.

16 National Archives, WORK 25/20. Copies of drawings for the restaurant are at WORK 25/86.

17 The cancellation had occurred by 20 July 1950, when it was reported at a meeting of the Festival of Britain Architecture Council; National Archives, WORK 25/49 FBA (50) 6.

2 Parterre

There was, however, a relatively happy ending to the Festival of Britain project. Some time after the building of the restaurant had been cancelled, the Festival organisers telephoned Leonard Manasseh to ask him whether he would be able to take on a consolation prize: the design of some lavatories on the South Bank site. Manasseh's first reaction was an irritated 'of course not'. He mentioned the invitation, however, to his landlord, who told him not to fall prey to injured pride. 'Don't be ridiculous,' he said, 'they are being helpful'. After all, even lavatories would bring in the fees that would pay the rent.[1]

In fact, the lavatory project grew to include a prominent water tower, a small café, an electric sub-station and a large rooftop terrace. The '51 Bar, as the project was named, was located near the entrance to the site, by the River Thames at the County Hall end.

above **The '51 Bar, South Bank, London, photographed by Millar and Harris just before the official opening of the Festival of Britain.**
opposite **The Rotork Works from the east.**

above top A daytime view of the bar, at the County Hall end of the Festival site.
above The Rosie Lee Café at the 'Live Architecture' exhibition in Poplar, London, 1951, designed by Leonard Manasseh with Sadie Speight.

At the centre of the composition was a two-storey brick pavilion with a brick base, and a butterfly roof above a partially open upper storey: this housed the bar, reached by a steel staircase. At the landward end, an airy tower made up from narrow black steel sections rose more than twice as high. Just below the top there was a 23,000-litre (5,000-gallon) water tank, which supplied George Grenfell-Baines's and Heinz J. Reifenberg's Power and Production Pavilion next door. The lavatories began on the storey below the bar level and continued north towards the river, and the terrace was above them, camouflaged by columns, canopies and bunting. The whole of the structure was breezy and colourful; it was decorated with prominent Festival lettering, and inside there were pretty lamps and stools – with some of the furniture designed by Manasseh himself. Its longest-lasting feature was a sculpture that stood at the foot of its stairs. Entitled Youth, it was an attenuated female nude by the sculptor Daphne Hardy Henrion, whose most recent claim to fame at the time had been the rescue of her lover Arthur Koestler's manuscript of *Darkness at Noon*. Manasseh managed to claim the sculpture when the exhibition closed in September 1951. Some fragments of the bar and its furnishings survived to be displayed at the 'A Tonic to the Nation' exhibition at the Victoria and Albert Museum in 1976, but the publication of the same name that accompanied the exhibition, and which until recently provided the most detailed description of the Festival of Britain, wrongly gives the impression that the bar was itself Manasseh's competition-winning scheme.[2]

The execution even of this small scheme made Manasseh a member of a group of architects who henceforth played a considerable part in finding him work: not only his close friends Philip Powell and Hidalgo Moya, but also Leslie Martin, Hugh Casson, Basil Spence and the wartime AA head Frederick Gibberd. All of these helped out in the days when large public projects were commissioned, like private ones, on the basis of a personal recommendation from an established practitioner. In the short term, Casson gave Manasseh a role on the Festival's travelling exhibition, while Martin found Manasseh enough work to support his newly established independence, suggesting that he help out with some of the small projects that his (Martin's) wife, the architect Sadie Speight, was unable to undertake because of illness. As well as being one of the few women architects in the public eye, Speight was an interior designer and product designer – she had been a founder member of the Design Research Association – and she had also co-authored with her husband *The Flat Book*, a guide to modern design products available in pre-war Britain. Her association with Manasseh was thus a promising and useful one for him. The first of these projects was a building that formed part of the Festival's Live Architecture Exhibition, Gibberd's model Lansbury Estate at Poplar in the East End of London. The exhibition was intended to demonstrate what new urban architecture would be like in the age of public ownership and development. Here they built the Rosie Lee Café in a demotic but lively and colourful Scandinavian style. By contrast, their Gay Kaye handbag shop at 4 New Bond Street in the West End more closely resembled an art gallery, with its minimalist glass frontage and bold shop name in a translucent panel above the door. The interior had very little in the way of

fittings: mostly glass cases with steel frames and legs, and a tall shelving unit at the centre of the sales floor. As the *Architects' Journal* noted at the time, the design turned the whole of the shop into a showcase that faced the street.[3]

Not long after the Festival closed, Casson invited Manasseh to design one of the interiors for the prestigious Time and Life office building on the corner of New Bond Street and Bruton Street, designed by Michael Rosenauer and incorporating work by several of the Festival's designers and artists. By contrast, another project from this period was a bowls pavilion with a brightly coloured interior for the London County Council (LCC), off Hilly Fields Crescent in Lewisham, which still stands. After the Festival win, Manasseh had invited Ian Baker, a former housemate and recent AA graduate, to work alongside him, opening an office in Buckingham Street off the Strand. These projects from the earliest days of their partnership already established many of the characteristics of their future practice together, from their professional connections and collaborations to their pavilion-like architecture, their sparkling and crisp interiors and their imaginative use of standardised components such as glazed boxes with narrow black steel frames.

above **Gay Kaye in Bond Street, designed by Leonard Manasseh with Sadie Speight.**

above top LCC Bowls Pavilion, Lewisham, London, designed by Leonard Manasseh with Sadie Speight.
above The House of Richard, a pen shop in Liverpool Street, London, designed by Leonard Manasseh with Sadie Speight.

Partnership with Ian Baker

Manasseh's partnership with Ian Baker was unquestionably the richest of all the
associations that he made through the AA. It was also to be the longest-lasting
relationship in both their lives. Without 'wonderful' Baker, said Manasseh, two months
before Baker's death in May in 2010, 'nothing would have been achieved. He was the
best partner that any architect could wish for'.[4] Baker had in fact begun his studies at
the department of art at the University College of Wales at Aberystwyth, to which he
had been admitted thanks to the one enormous measured drawing of a neo-classical
building he had presented at his interview. In 1941, he transferred to the AA, to the
unit run by E. R. Jarrett and A. Gavin, and he continued until called up for war service
at the end of his second year in 1943.[5] He spent three years with the Air Ministry
Experimental Station, partly in Libya and Palestine, recording his time there with
topographical drawings and portraits of airmen. On returning to the AA he left his
mark on the school's publications, drawing cartoons and incidental decorations. For
a while he helped support himself by drawing advertising material and book covers.
He completed his studies in 1949 and took a job with Grey Wornum, immediately
creating the published perspective sketches for the latter's Parliament Square scheme.[6]

above top **A young Ian Baker.**

above left top An airman drawn by Ian Baker during his wartime service in the RAF.
above right top A landscape near Tripoli, drawn by Ian Baker in 1946.
above Ian Baker's student project for British Council offices.

His partnership with Manasseh had been kindled after meeting again at Philip Powell's home in The Little Boltons, and for a while in 1946–8 they shared a house with several others at 12 Neville Terrace nearby in South Kensington.[7]

Baker's family background was, like Manasseh's, in commerce. He was born in Westcliff-on-Sea, near Southend in Essex, on 23 May 1923 to parents who owned a chain of south-coast ladies' clothing shops. His mother managed them, and so he was sent away to board at Mill Hill School. He also shared with Manasseh a great interest in and enjoyment of machinery without, likewise, having much of a mastery of numbers or of mechanical processes himself. From the start, the two men worked so inseparably that staff found it hard to decide who had done what. Their styles of drawing, although distinguishable to those who knew them well, were extremely similar and Manasseh's son Phin remembers that on occasions they would sometimes add to or finish each other's work.

above top The Smithsons, thinly disguised as 'Mervyn Biro' and 'Anna Dyze', drawn by Ian Baker for the AA student journal *Plan*, 1948.
above left 'Sir Frank Ashlar OBE RA PPIBA', another caricature by Ian Baker for *Plan*.
above right 'Randym Rubbel ARIBA' and 'Charles Fletton Sandface FRIBA', by Ian Baker for *Plan*.

Manasseh was certainly the public face of the partnership, and was more comfortable with some clients than Baker was, and yet for a brief period near the start of their professional relationship Baker, sometimes assisted by his wife Patricia, was in command of the office. This arose because in October 1953, Manasseh departed to Singapore to establish a simultaneous partnership there with another AA connection James Cubitt, already the partner in London of Manasseh's old friend and former classmate Stefan Buzás. The idea was that Manasseh would be able to draw on his family connections to establish a sizeable office in the colony. This adventure began with the modest job of converting an office for a firm of stockbrokers, but before long the opportunity arose, through his sister Sylvia, to design some housing for the Sultan of Brunei.[8] As it turned out, however, Manasseh had to return in the summer of 1954 to look after his young children after the departure of his first wife, and the Cubitt partnership seems to have persisted only on paper.[9] It was presumably because of this period abroad that Baker at last formally became Manasseh's partner in the practice, fulfilling a promise that Manasseh had originally made after his competition win.[10]

Neither architect, although often admiring the work of friends and contemporaries, ever referred to any designer other than Le Corbusier as an inspiration. Manasseh's admiration was already there in 1943, when together with Buzás he wrote a short illustrated article entitled 'time, trees and architecture' for the *Architectural Review* in what turned out to be one of its most memorable issues. Here, the young enthusiasts praised the Petite Maison de Week-end, the prototype for the Maisons Jaoul, at

above Ian Baker photographed by John Deakin, mid-1950s.

La-Celle-St-Cloud south of Paris, already eight years old.[11] Manasseh took his second wife Sarah, whom he married in 1957, to Roquebrune-Cap Martin for their honeymoon, close to the Master's *cabanon*. Many years later, he enthusiastically introduced architects to an edition of Le Corbusier's sketchbooks as 'a document of the greatest architectural and historical importance'.[12] Like most architects discussing others, Manasseh never said what exactly it was that he found so inspiring – although he did say on that occasion that the sketchbooks were 'evocative and mysterious, hovering on the brink of revelation'. This quality is reflected in his own drawings, many of which are expectant scenes set under bright orange suns or moons. In this later article, Manasseh retold one of his favourite stories: he had been on holiday in Provence when Le Corbusier drowned in 1966. Baker came over to see him and related the news of the death, adding: 'You're on your own now.' Baker, when asked about influences on his own work in 2009, merely gestured silently to the Corbusier volumes on his bookshelves.[13]

Not for nothing was the partnership's telegraphic address 'CUBEMAN LONDON'. Manasseh and Baker liked simple geometrical shapes: squares, pyramids and triangles, with crisp arrises and minimal frames. Manasseh disliked pastiche of any kind, quoting with satisfaction in 1981 a joke of Peter Aldington's: 'Do not prostitute your architecture or you will catch vernacular disease.'[14] However, he admired the

above **Untitled painting by Leonard Manasseh, October 1971.**

unselfconscious vernacular that had historically emerged for simple building types, which used 'the commoner materials' in new ways, and he liked the geometrical forms of old farmhouses in Brittany and Provence. His own houses sometimes come close to imitating them.[15] Yet his pitched-roof houses cannot be mistaken for pastiche vernacular because of their sharp, minimal detailing around the eaves.

Designing private houses

Because of their closeness in working together it is sometimes difficult to distinguish the partners' different hands in the design of a job, although a certain degree of demarcation can be recognised. Manasseh, for example, was the principal designer of the partnership's private houses. Though few in number, it was these that in the early days received a relatively large amount of publicity and drew attention to the firm.

Soon after establishing the practice, Manasseh designed a house in Pulborough, West Sussex, for the parents of a Fleet Air Arm friend, John Wright.[16] This was followed in 1952 by a house for his solicitor cousin Philip Manasseh, his wife Renée and their two young children on a bomb-site in Campden Hill Road, Kensington – something of a family compound, since Manasseh's aunt and uncle lived four houses further up. The five-bedroom house was built when post-war restrictions were still in place, which meant that the basement, on which the two storeys sat, had to be left half-unexcavated and unused. Although small, the building had a number of relatively grand features, the most impressive of which was a curved open staircase in front of a tall and wide window adjacent to the front door; this immediately gave

above left **51 Campden Hill Road, Kensington, London, for Philip and Renée Manasseh, 1952.**
above right **Looking out from the hall.**

a cheerful, open feeling to anyone who came in. The house had a separate dining room for 'a great deal of formal entertaining', as *House & Garden* put it, and the sitting room had a shallow bow window facing the street with a little balcony for the dressing room above it. At the front, an arched steel hood above the front door convinced the freeholders, the Phillimore Estate, that the design was not too modern for the area, and at the back there was a canopied terrace. Manasseh designed the interior joinery, including a cabinet the length of the sitting-room wall, built-in bedside units and bathrooms lined in Vitrolite, the coloured glass manufactured in Britain by Pilkington Brothers. The walls inside were painted white, but Renée Manasseh liked to point out that the changing direction of the light and the bold colours of the curtains and carpet within created a continuously varying interior. This house has, interestingly, survived in better condition than almost all Manasseh's others; although it is a modest building, in an area where the value of a plot of land can exceed the cost of any house built on it, subsequent owners have found it so pleasant to live in – and so good for parties – that it remains much as it was, in a context now dominated by Sir Basil Spence's uncompromising town hall opposite.

Next came a series of three houses designed towards the end of the 1950s on the plot of a large Victorian house called The Lawns, at 16 South Grove, Highgate. The extensive garden ran down towards Highgate Cemetery to the south. In December 1953, *Architectural Design* had published two proposals by Manasseh: one for a 'house in Highgate', and another for a much smaller one 'in North London'. The circumstances of their design have not been discovered, but they are worth noting because of the contrast between them and the houses that Manasseh eventually built on the Lawns site some six years later. The 'house in Highgate' project in particular was a conventional design for the period, similar in style to that of the well-regarded house of the same year by Michael Ventris in Parfitt Close, near North End in Hampstead. These two, and Kenneth Capon's almost contemporary cottage opposite the latter, all shared an unapologetically Scandinavian style with low-pitched gables. Yet each of the three houses Manasseh completed on the Highgate site was quite unlike any of these, and indeed quite unlike its two new neighbours. On the site of The Lawns itself, and reusing some of its foundations, he designed a two-storey, flat-roofed house sharing some features with the one in Kensington. The south-facing garden front of the house was quite different, however. The ground floor was glazed from one end to the other between brick piers, lighting adjoining sitting and dining rooms. Above the windows ran a chain of shallow-arched concrete beams, a memento from the Petite Maison de Week-end, or by this time, the more recent Maisons Jaoul. The brick piers continued up through the floor above, and there was a recessed balcony on the bedroom storey. The result looked very unlike a house but the inside, which was extensively photographed for the *Architect & Building News*, was again cheerful and comfortable. The house was remodelled and enveloped in glass for Sir John Sorrell at the end of the 20th century in an award-winning scheme by Eldridge Smerrin.

The two further plots to the south of The Lawns, on the site of its gardens, were

Existing Basements.

Best Wishes for Christmas & The New Year from

Leonard **MANASSEH** & Partners

Leonard....

accessible from a new lane thanks to the development of the adjoining site, where Manasseh's friend Anthony Cox was already completing his own house.[17] When the owner of The Lawns offered the plots for sale, Manasseh himself bought the south- ernmost one to build a house for his family: his wife Sarah, and his children Alan, Zac, Amos and Becky, soon to be followed by Phin. The result, 6 Bacon's Lane of 1957–9, is possibly the building most associated with its architect; it was widely published, and continues to be photographed and written about up to the present day. Unlike any of the Scandinavian-type houses, this compact yellow-brick building

above top The garden front of The Lawns, Highgate, London, on the office Christmas card for 1958.
above *House & Garden* visits 6 Bacon's Lane, March 1962.

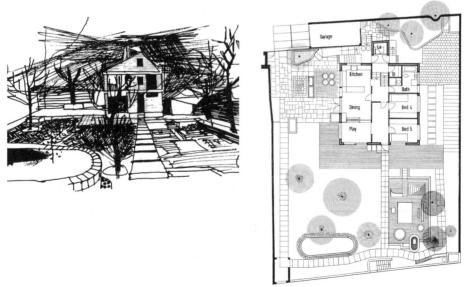

above top 6 Bacon's Lane, Highgate, London, from the south-west. The dormer indicates the position of the studio.

above left A sketch of the garden elevation.

above right The ground-floor plan of the house, with Leonard Manasseh's garden design.

has a tall, asymmetrical gable facing the garden; this dominates its composition and establishes its principal planning idea. Flying out from the ridge is a dormer window which lights a roof-level studio, and this overlooks the first-floor drawing room at the south-west corner of the house. Entry is at a half-landing on the northern side; stairs lead up to the drawing room and main bedroom, and down to an open kitchen, dining and playrooms, and the children's bedrooms. This is a tight, formal composition with very little circulation space achieving great sophistication within a covenanted restriction limiting the design to two main storeys. The plan itself is a 9.14 metre (30 foot) square, with a careful use of squares and golden sections in the design of all its openings. The deep concrete string-courses – in fact, the edges of the floor slabs – and an *in situ* decorative concrete panel on the garden side give the house a much more assertive air than that of any of Manasseh's other houses. The bricks were second-hand, from a demolished church in Southgate, adding texture to the building.

The house attracted considerable attention right from the start, in local and national newspapers and magazines: writers were fascinated by the upstairs sitting room with its tall open ceiling, the studio that overlooked it, and in particular its marble paving

above **The first-floor drawing room at 6 Bacon's Lane, overlooked by the studio (at the top left of the photograph).**

from slabs found in Portsmouth and originally intended for washstands. Manasseh himself described his home as 'modern and adventurous' in an article in the *London Evening Standard* that had the startling heading 'NOW – A Modernist Speaks Out'; and 'Alice Hope's Home Column' in the *Daily Mail* applauded the fact that it had 'no dark corners or winding stairs'.[18] When first photographed the house seemed austere, but in time Manasseh's collection of paintings filled the walls with strong and balanced patches of colour, implying that this composition had been planned from the beginning. He designed all the internal joinery, including the cedar of Lebanon panelling and

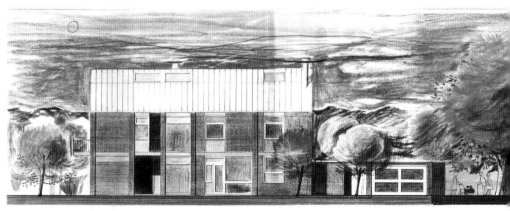

above top **The drawing room and studio at 6 Bacon's Lane, Highgate, drawn by Leonard Manasseh.**
above across to opposite page **3 Bank Lane, Roehampton, London, for Peter and Roseann Rea, 1962–5.**

cupboards which line the main bedroom. He also designed the garden, carefully positioning the Hardy Henrion statue from the '51 Bar.[19] Manasseh then designed the third house on the original Lawns site, a bungalow for the Singers (Gwen Singer was disabled) on the middle plot. This has been substantially remodelled inside, but its exterior appearance has hardly changed. A further family residence was the Rea House of 1962–5, for his cousin Roseann and her husband Peter, on the other side of London at 3 Bank Lane in the north-west corner of Roehampton. This had another asymmetrically gabled roof, this time with an attic lit by clerestory windows below the top ridge.

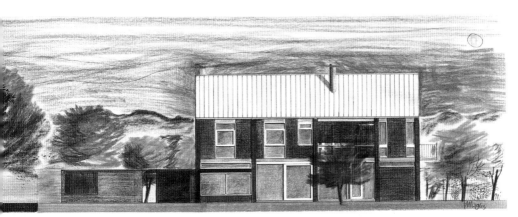

WEST

above top **6 Bacon's Lane from the garden, with Youth in the foreground.**

The plan was an extended version of that seen at The Lawns, with most of the ground floor taken up by dining and sitting rooms that face the garden. The roof was clad in aluminium, which means that it sparkles in the sun and is easy to make out on the descent into Heathrow Airport. Finally, Manasseh built a speculative terrace of three houses for his mother on the corner of Broadlands Road and Grange Road in Highgate in 1966. These have the sawtooth roof profile that was becoming a recognisable characteristic of his work.[20]

Two major houses designed by Manasseh formed a pair, and indeed shared a landscaped garden. Drum House and Courtyards, off River Lane in Petersham near Richmond in Surrey, were designed and built from 1964 to 1967. In this case the two owners came to Manasseh together, having previously asked friends for recommendations for the most exciting architect in England.[21] Drum House, designed for the Carr Jones family, was a large, long house with an inside swimming pool. Courtyards, for the family of the film director Richard Lester (then making *Help!* with the Beatles), was smaller, wrapped around an open, internal glazed atrium. Both houses were timber-clad with large windows in squares and rectangles completely filling the steel frame in most elevations. The sitting rooms of both were double-height, with fully glazed upper levels, and the roofs were either flat or had very steep monopitches or asymmetrical gables. The two houses, which were a prestigious commission and expensively finished, seemed almost to exaggerate Manasseh's characteristic design features:

above **Drum House, Petersham, Surrey, 1964–7, photographed by John Donat.**

Drum House had very tall narrow chimneys, and a tiny oriel window with a triangular plan. The shared garden, designed by John Brookes, was itself the subject of an article in *House & Garden* as it reached early maturity in 1976, although in general the owners tried to avoid publicity for their homes – possibly unfortunately for Manasseh, who was never again offered the opportunity to design a house on this scale. Courtyards has survived, but Drum House, following some remodelling, has been demolished.

Another private client who found Manasseh through recommendation was John Curtis, who in the early 1970s wanted to build a house near his wife's parents' home at Lower Radley, just east of Abingdon in Berkshire (now Oxfordshire). He sought advice through his wife Lou's connections to the Cadogan Estate, the Chelsea landowners. Their suggestions included Manasseh and a young Norman Foster. After interviewing the two, the Curtises chose Manasseh, and never regretted it. The house was erected in 1973–4, and the relationship with their architect was a particularly warm one. This was a small house with a conservatory that rose up to the roof through two storeys, the glazing narrowing as it ascended. Inside there was a spiral staircase, a form which

above **55 Lower Radley, Abingdon, Oxfordshire, completed in 1974 for John and Lou Curtis.**

Manasseh had recently added to his characteristic vocabulary. The house still stands, but has been substantially remodelled by later owners. Other houses designed by Manasseh include Lane's End, the warden's house of 1966–8 at Beaford – an arts centre established under the aegis of Dartington Hall – with triple-height spaces and spiral stairs; and a house for the Craven family near Blandford Forum in Dorset. At Sandwich Bay in East Kent, Manasseh designed a bungalow called the Lighthouse for one of the proprietors of Wilmot-Breeden, the car accessories manufacturers, perhaps in the hope that a large works project would follow.

Just before the arrival of the commission for the two houses at Petersham, Manasseh designed the first of three buildings for sites in the South of France which express very clearly his enthusiasm for the simple geometrical forms of local farm buildings. This first house was for the banker and art patron Mike Behrens, for a site at La Vigie, at Cap la Cavalaire near St Tropez on the Côte d'Azur between Marseilles and Nice. The client lost interest because of delays in installing local service infrastructures, so the 17-bedroom house was not built. However, Manasseh's drawings and model for it appear in the number of *Arena*, the AA journal, that introduced him as President in 1964. The similarity between the scheme and a photograph taken by its designer of what

above **The Craven family house at Brickwheat Bottom, near Blandford Forum, 1966.**

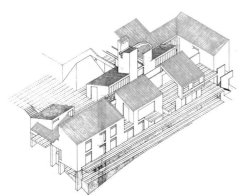

he called 'the "with it" vernacular of Brittany' is remarkable: both have colliding steep gables and a tall, thin chimney.[22] The other two buildings, much smaller but equally dramatic, were designed and built by Manasseh for his family as holiday homes. The first of these was perched on a precipice above the village of Champeau, to the west of the town of Merindol north of Marseilles. Manasseh's idea here was to use a modern vernacular – rendered concrete blocks with a pantiled roof, the normal way that most cheap building was done locally.[23] The house had a simple plan consisting of an open ground floor, a pair of bedrooms with a terrace, and a top-floor gallery. The building's profile, however, was a striking wedge shape, with apertures cut cleanly into the walls without sills, projections or ornament of any kind. In the late 1990s, when Manasseh was in his mid-eighties, he designed a further family summer house in a similar style at Paziols, north-west of Perpignan – his final project.

above top The Lighthouse, Sandwich Bay, Kent, 1967.
above left La Vigie, near St Tropez, France, for Mike Behrens, mid-1960s: axonometric projection.
above right La Vigie: model.

The partnership also designed a number of small multiple-unit private housing developments, usually with Baker as lead designer. The first of these was a tall narrow block of flats, the remodelling of a bomb-damaged house with a new block attached, on the corner of Courtfield Road and Ashburn Place in West London. It was demolished in the course of the recent Gloucester Road underground station development.[24] John Newman's *Buildings of England* guide to *North East and East Kent* described the partnership's Riverside Close of 1965–6, in the village of Bridge near Canterbury and designed by the project architect Robert Huddleston, as 'quite exceptionally good, the rarity which should and could be the norm'.[25] The terraced houses have original and versatile floor plans centred on an open dining hall.[26] Following an initiative by Elizabeth Chesterton, the partnership's planning consultant, Baker designed a small group of houses at Pearce's Yard in Grantchester as residences for fellows of King's College, Cambridge, in 1969–71.[27] Both the last-named developments have survived and their pantiled roofs, sculptural brickwork and neat garaging arrangements reveal their common parentage. In both cases, though, their subtlety has been compromised by unsympathetic plastic window frames and mullions. Baker designed a small house on Castlenau in Barnes, in West London, now altered, and the practice made many minor alterations to existing properties.[28]

above **The Manasseh family holiday house at Champeau, Provence.**

Jeremy Fry and Rotork

Of all the connections that Manasseh made during his career at the AA, Jeremy Fry (1924–2005) was probably the most unexpected and the most remarkable. Later known to the public as a major supporter of the arts in the city of Bath and beyond; as a figure in royal circles; and, by the 1990s, as the mentor of the inventor James Dyson; the endlessly energetic and creative Fry was a member of the chocolate-manufacturing family in Bristol. He had been Manasseh's student at the AA before his studies were interrupted by service in the Royal Air Force during the Second World War, and after he returned he had been the landlord of the architectural commune at Neville Terrace. He was, however, like his older brother David, drawn to engineering rather than architecture. Indeed the family is still best known in some circles for the motoring exploits of their young days, including the invention of the 'Freikaiserwagen', a record-breaking vehicle resembling a cross between a car and a motorcycle that David Fry and his cousin Joe built in 1936.[29] 'Handsome, charismatic, with blinding green eyes', in the words of his friend and business associate Andy Garnett, Jeremy Fry started work in 1954 as a product designer for his brother's Frenchay Products Ltd, a company which designed and built specialist prototypes for the aviation industry in Station Road at Kingswood near Bristol.[30]

above Fellows' houses for King's College, Cambridge, at Grantchester, Cambridgeshire, 1969–71, drawn by Ian Baker.

Fry had idolised Manasseh, and around the time he started working for his brother the opportunity arose for him to recommend his former teacher as the architect of new offices to front the Frenchay works. The layout of the building was simple, with few partitions within the narrow spaces, but the delicate elegance of its detailing was remarkable for an engineering works. Its steel frame was faced with a 30.48 metre (100 foot) curtain wall of windows and panels divided by narrow stanchions. At the northern end a porch canopy, a large version of that on The Lawns, was thrust out above the entrance door and steps. Visitors entered a brightly coloured reception area on the raised ground floor where the open-tread staircase was dark green with white edges, and the ceiling pale blue. The walls were yellow and cadmium red. Panels of white

above top **Jeremy Fry, photographed by Snowdon in the early 1980s.**
above **The Frenchay works at Kingswood, Bristol, 1955.**

ceramic tiles made patterns on the floor, providing a base for a regency couch, the only piece of furniture in the space. The remarkably glossy showcase-like effect, enhanced by Festival-type lettering on glazed panels, was published in colour in *Architectural Design*, and the details of the building appeared in the *Architects' Journal*. Both publications enjoyed the boardroom, designed, the architects said, 'to be as workmanlike as possible' but which was dominated by two large photomontages. One was of an Avro Vulcan, the RAF's recent delta-wing bomber, soaring through clouds, and the other more whimsical, with a hot air balloon and enlarged sketches.

In 1957, Jeremy Fry left his brother to set up a business under the name of Rotork that designed and manufactured sealed actuators – that is, electro-mechanical components that can regulate the operation of pipework valves. The significance of Fry's work lay in his design of the sealing: up to then, any valve that was opened for maintenance or repair was susceptible to fouling or damage. At first, Fry worked from Widcombe Manor, his baroque mansion in Bath, but the success of the actuators, which greatly reduced maintenance costs for their users, and their adoption in a large state project in France meant that he soon required a works building. Over the next 20 years Manasseh created a complex, eventually housing some 250 workers, on a site beside the River Avon to the north-west of Bath city centre.

To start with, he designed a simple works structure with five parallel sheds to house the assembly line, fronted on the river side by a single-storey timber-framed office and reception building. The company moved in during 1962, but soon afterwards a substantial extension was required for a finished goods and packing room of equal floor area to the existing building. The extension needed not only an unobstructed floor space of about 1,400 square metres (15,000 square feet) but also to be able to support weights of over five tonnes suspended from the ceiling. Together with the engineers Felix J. Samuely & Partners, Manasseh and Baker designed a building dominated by a triodetic roof; that is, a structural space frame on a triangular module, supported by only two column. These rose up into the apexes of tall glazed pyramids, which lit the area together with angled clerestory windows around the whole of the perimeter. Raising the prefabricated triodetic structure on site took only 25 minutes, according to the *Architectural Review*; and it was during that time that Dyson, then a student at the Royal College of Art, first turned up at the works to meet Fry. The outer walls were faced with Bath stone at the request of the local planning authority. In addition, the offices were now extended towards the river, and their south-facing windows were very soon fitted with long canvas canopies that could be extended down to the ground. In 1973, the Farrell/Grimshaw Partnership completed an extension including a large new reception area, but Leonard Manasseh & Partners were invited back the same year to carry out further work for Rotork. The packing area was extended eastwards, and part of it was converted into offices with projecting windows towards the river; the offices gained an extra floor; and fixed louvred sun screens replaced the fabric canopies. The building is admired and appreciated by those who work in it today.

above top One of the two columns supporting the roof of the finished goods and packing area at Rotork.
above The Rotork works seen from the east in 2010.

The partnership also designed a number of domestic projects for the Frys, two of which were unusual conversions. In 1984, Jeremy Fry moved into the former brewery that the partnership had used as a branch office at Freshford, near Bath. The drawing office became a gigantic drawing room with a leather floor (a Fry trademark) that provided a suitable backdrop for his collection of objects and paintings. A glamorous spiral staircase with a brass balustrade led up from the entrance hall into a library. For David Fry, Manasseh and Baker restored and remodelled a ruinous late 14th-century keep called Garth Castle near Keltneyburn in the north of Perthshire, said to have been a stronghold of Alexander Stewart, the 'Wolf of Badenoch'. The castle was a massive stone structure, with walls about two metres (6 feet 6 inches) thick and a few small windows, and it consisted of a single open space above a vaulted dungeon. The partnership turned this into one of their most splendid interiors. The basement was converted into a bathroom and guest room, and the whole of the rest of the space became a living room with a sleeping balcony at first-floor level, all lit by a large glass-fibre rooflight high up above a second upper gallery. The sitting-room floor was paved in white marble. The dining table, also topped with marble, was cantilevered from the

above **The offices at Rotork today: workers look out directly towards the River Avon.**

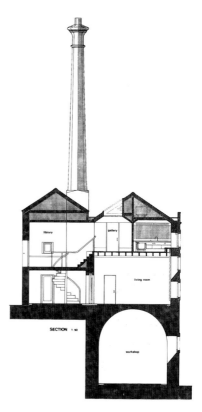

wall and had an internal heating element – in fact, Fry left the electrical underfloor
heating on all year to make the castle habitable. A few pieces of furniture were carefully
arranged around the room. There were red Magistretti dining chairs set in front of
olive green tweed curtains, and an Eames lounge chair and ottoman, artfully disposed
for the camera. Upstairs, the walls were so massive that the beds could be set into the
thickness of them. The architects designed furniture and various fittings and gadgets,
including freestanding enclosed kitchen and bathroom units. In 1965, José Manser
wrote about Garth for *Ideal Home* in an article accompanied by suitably luscious photographs by Sam Lambert. The partnership also remodelled a house in Bath, 1 Queen's
Parade, for David's wife Joy, and made designs for a boathouse in Feock in Cornwall for
Jeremy.

above left Freshford brewery, near Bath, after conversion in to a house: the library landing, with the gallery
beyond.
above right Freshford brewery: section.

Art boys or system boys?

In his presidential address to the A A of 1964, Manasseh emphasised the importance of
bringing together the 'art boys', the one-off creative artists, and the 'system boys', the
rationalists – and this was something he tried to do in his own work.[31] The two types
of project he principally undertook – factories and works offices on the one hand, and
elegant interior fittings on the other – exemplified the dichotomy that troubled him.
He attempted to solve it by reversing the expected architectural language in each case.
He gave his industrial buildings something of the delicate quality of exhibition architecture, with glazed panels within fine metal frames, whereas his houses are chunkier,
with sculptural forms punctured by deep apertures. The sequences of monopitch roofs
that appear in his domestic architecture are, of course, forms normally associated with
factories. Thus, Jeremy Fry was the perfect client for Manasseh's continuing attempts
to reconcile the two sides: Fry was an engineer, but he was also a connoisseur and a
supporter of contemporary arts.

Manasseh had little sense of the technical processes of engineering, and perhaps

above Garth Castle, Perthshire, photographed by Sam Lambert for *Ideal Home* in 1965.

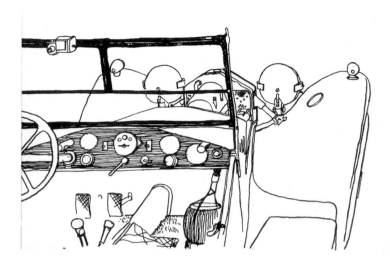

for that reason his interest in expressing mechanical processes through artistic means is important to his work. He believed that architecture should aim to suit modern life, so if the latter was full of machines then the former, its overall form and its ornament, should express it. He designed structural systems, such as glazed steel frames, to be as beautiful as they were practical, but he also used them to signal the fact that their historical origin as pieces of design lay in their function rather than in their appearance. They represent functionalism in an elegant way, through elements that resemble moving shafts, struts and joints in a mechanical assembly, rather than actually being strictly functional. It is possible too that Manasseh, in common with many architects, felt that his lack of mastery over the technical side of engineering was something that needed to be compensated for. These concerns were in the air at the time: it was in a lecture in Cambridge in 1959 that the novelist and engineer C. P. Snow described the damage caused to society as a whole by the intellectual divide between 'The Two Cultures', the scientists and the literary people. When Manasseh raised the subject of this divide in his presidential address, his friend Diana Rowntree, who had studied at the AA in the years immediately before he did, included in her formal response the observation that 'What intrigues me tonight is to listen to an artist like Leonard Manasseh disposing once and for all of the fallacy that our future lies in the arts. But then this, our AA, is Paradox Hall.'[32] It is interesting that some of the students at the AA who opposed the merger of their school with Imperial College saw the whole idea of reconciling the arts with the sciences within a regulated academic framework as being something that belonged to an older generation.[33]

However, the other reason Manasseh was so interested in this theme was surely the fact that at the time most of his projects seemed to fall clearly into either the 'art'

above A Manasseh sketch of a 1930's car, published by the AA journal *Arena* in June 1964.

category or the 'system' one. The practice carried out a number of works buildings in the 'Frenchay style' in the mid-1950s. These included a headquarters for the electronics company Wayne Kerr, near Tolworth in Surrey, now gone, followed by another building for the same firm at Bognor Regis, completed in 1964. According to a list included with his biographical file at the RIBA in March 1968, he also designed a large set of offices and laboratories in Turkey in 1961. His industrial buildings were elegant, but they were also systematic in the sense that the frame of the building and the use of modular components determined their appearance and plan. Yet at the same time, the partnership was being commissioned to design restaurants and other prestige one-off projects. In the mid-1950s, Manasseh had remodelled the high-class La Reserve restaurant, in Gerrard Street in Soho, creating the desired sense of luxury through large expanses of rich colour and Italian touches. An arched suspended ceiling papered in gold covered the old plaster cornices in the main dining space, and the room was painted the colour of 'the bloom on black grapes'.[34] The seats were crimson, and the walls seaweed green. A Fornasetti-type enlargement of a French renaissance print screened the stairs from the red-ceilinged entrance hall, and the bar with its

above **Wayne Kerr at Tolworth, Surrey: a project typical of the partnership's industrial work.**

Ponti chairs and classical marble heads was decorated in black and white. Nearly all of the fittings and furniture were designed by the architects.[35] It was, one critic wrote, 'a modern restaurant of the highest order'.[36] When Geoffrey Scarsbrook, eventually a partner, joined the practice at the beginning of the 1960s, he designed several restaurant interiors of this type, including the Belvedere in Holland Park and the Hook Line and Sinker in Baker Street – both upmarket ventures for J. Lyons – and then the interior of the Looking Glass restaurant on the top floor of T. P. Bennett & Son's Royal Lancaster Hotel at Lancaster Gate.[37]

The luxury car is an object that brings together the creative artist with the engineer, and cars and car components became a continuing theme in Manasseh's work. It was appropriate that in 1960 the *Architectural Review* turned to the partnership to come up with ideas for how an ideal motorway service station should look in the era of the M1 – opened in November 1959. The published design shows a walled but open pedestrian plaza with seats, trees, kiosks and public telephones between two car parks, alongside a restaurant and café buildings. The scheme makes an interesting harbinger of the pioneering work Manasseh and Baker did later for Lord Montagu of Beaulieu, especially since Manasseh thought that architects in general did not care enough about the beauty of mechanical objects. Joe Hayward, in the mid-1960s a 20-year-old articled pupil in Preston, clearly remembers Manasseh coming to the North Lancashire Society of Architects to give a talk about the National Motor Museum project, still some way off.

above **Hook Line and Sinker, an upmarket J. Lyons restaurant in Baker Street, London.**

above top Hook Line and Sinker.
above The Looking Glass restaurant on the top floor of the Royal Lancaster Hotel, Bayswater Road, London: the bar rail (left) was clad in pink leather.

Manasseh wanted to emphasise how important it was to him that the architects were not seen by their clients as being just a 'lot of swifties down from London', as he himself put it, churning out designs without thinking them through. Manasseh seemed very avuncular, says Hayward, an opinion shared by everyone who met him. As for his view of himself, he was, when younger, perpetually 'dreamy' and 'optimistic'.[38]

Rutherford School

A further large project was designed in the 1950s, and this turned out to be one of the dreamiest and most optimistic of all the partnership's buildings. In 1957, the LCC commissioned it to design Rutherford Secondary School for 800 boys, in Bell Street in Marylebone, close to Edgware Road Bakerloo line underground station.[39] The site included the school's old premises, the former Bellfield board school, at its south-east corner: the idea was that the pupils would move directly from the old building into the new one without interruption before the former was demolished, and the area left for the new school was L-shaped.

The general plan of the partnership's proposal was unremarkable in the context of contemporary LCC school-building. A single three-storey block nearly 90 metres (290 feet) long, fronting Penfold Street to the west, contained classrooms, a library, house rooms (that is, community spaces for the children), various offices and a caretaker's flat. A cross-axial link connected this block with the second main structure: a glazed assembly hall with a bold pyramidal slate roof. To the north and south of the hall were

above **An ideal service station for the M1: a project by the partnership for the *Architectural Review*.**

a pair of gymnasiums lit by clerestory windows, separated from the long block by landscaped courts either side of the link building. The organisation of the spaces was thus a simple one.

The long block on Penfold Street took the form of an uninterrupted sequence of identical narrow bays made up from projecting narrow structural concrete mullions filled with Crittall windows and pale grey panels. There is an undeniable dynamism to it, enhanced by the sculptural forms on the roof: at the southern end there is a glazed conservatory with a monopitch roof for young botanists, and at the northern end a group of tall chimneys. The most striking rooftop object, however, is the large inverted pyramid above the entrance. This contains water tanks, but from some angles it balances the large upright pyramid of the assembly hall to its east. This conjunction today most obviously recalls the saucer and dome of Niemeyer's parliament buildings at Brasilia, but that project was itself constructed only in 1958–60 and no critic mentioned it.[40] The hall pyramid itself, sitting at the centre of a flat roof and meticulously detailed with secret flashings at the arrises, was the crispest of the many that Manasseh designed.[41]

The processional route from the front door to the hall is the architectural centre-piece of the building. The entrance is through a brick wall on the Penfold Street side, below the tanks. On crossing through from the street into a covered way, a private sculpture court is revealed on the right-hand side. Here, mysterious geometrical forms in concrete and granite, designed by Manasseh, are set between pools and trees. These would have been enjoyed only briefly by hurrying boys but at length by the headmaster, the school office and the medical rooms which overlooked them: 'the remains of some earlier civilization, perhaps?', one writer asked.[42] On entering the school, visitors were astonished to find the walls lined with marble – a boy-proof material. The stair strings were marble, too. One then continued ahead into the glazed link, passing there a sculpture called *The Tree of Knowledge* by Hubert Dalwood, and glimpsed the landscaped courtyards to the north and south.[43] In the assembly hall

above **Rutherford School, presented to the readers of the *Architectural Review* in November 1960.**

beyond, the pupils' seats were located in an area sunk just under a metre (3 feet 3 inches) into the floor in order not to distract from the magnificent open space under the pyramid and before the stage.

The materials and colours, and the incorporation of the artworks, left a strong impression on visitors. Diana Rowntree wrote about the building in the *Guardian* in July 1960, soon after it was completed. She thought the school was 'something rich and strange that defies all categories'. In particular, she enjoyed the rich colours of the interior. A scarlet beam was:

> *given dayglow brilliance against a clear green ceiling. There are murky colours, pre-Raphaelite colours, juvenile colour schemes like orange and yellow, and a very subtle juxtaposition of bright blue and navy blue. It is all a breath-taking change from the demure primary philosophy of school decoration – one red wall, one blue, and one yellow. The architects have had fun with this building, from the small doodle in stained glass up in the art room to the concrete sculptures that act as a foil to the machine aesthetics of the long façade.[44]*

There was extensive coverage of the building too in the *Architectural Review*, *Architectural Design*, *Interbuild* and *Official Architecture and Planning*.

above **The northern courtyard.**

Forty years later, Manasseh said he thought the school was 'in every way one of the best jobs ever designed' by the partnership.[45] It has had an interesting life. In 1980 Michael Marland, at the forefront of the community-school movement, became headmaster, and Rutherford became part of the North Westminster Community School. Marland invited Manasseh to carry out minor alterations. The complex was listed Grade II* in 1998, the first of the partnership's projects to receive this honour. Following the school's reopening in 2007 as the King Solomon Academy, a specialist science and mathematics school, alterations by the architect Ian Ritchie have taken place. In spite of the listing, the gymnasiums were demolished and replaced by new structures, and the courtyards have been remodelled. The rest of the building, however, has been sympathetically restored.

above left A toplit upper-floor corridor.
above right Stained glass in the art room. The window faces the setting sun.

Notes

1   Referred to in Manasseh BL interviews, Tape 3 Side A, but often repeated in family circles. National Archives, WORK 25/86, has detailed drawings for the prizewinning restaurant dated as late as May 1950 and for the new reduced scheme from August 1950, so the reformulation of the project must have occurred in late July or early August.

2   Elain Harwood & Alan Powers eds. *Twentieth Century Architecture*, Journal no. 6, The Festival of Britain, London, Twentieth Century Society, 2001.

3   *Architects' Journal*, 3 January 1952, pp12–13.

4   Telephone message to author, 10 March 2010.

5   Architectural Association Archives, A503.

6   *Architects' Journal*, 25 August 1949, p195.

7   Brian Lemesle 'Beak' Adams from the school-building department at Hertfordshire County Council, Geoffry Powell and Hidalgo Moya were also in the house at some point, as were two Crittall sisters: Sylvia Manasseh, 2 March 2010; Manasseh BL interviews, Tape 4 Side A.

8   Sources: Sylvia Manasseh, 2 March 2010; Manasseh BL interviews, Tape 4 Side A; Tony Chapman, 5 April 2010. This was a terrace of four timber houses, raised on stilts over a parking area with open stairs and balconies, near the Padang in central Brunei.

9   *Architect & Building News*, 16 August 1956, pp233–6, published a design for a hotel in Singapore by James Cubitt, Leonard Manasseh & Partners, not in a characteristic Manasseh style. The hotel was not built.

10   Manasseh BL interviews, Tape 3 Side B, which includes further information about the earliest days of the practice.

11   *Architectural Review*, August 1943, pp52–3. The number also includes the article by Pevsner on A. W. N. Pugin which is now considered to mark the turning point in the modern appreciation of the architect. Manasseh's first appearance in the *Architectural Review* was his illustration for its 'Rebuilding Britain' issue, April 1943, p86, which was afterwards used as the cover for the Architectural Press's exhibition booklet *Towards a New Britain*, Cheam, Architectural Press, 1943.

12   *RIBA Journal*, June 1981, pp12–13.

13   During the course of a conversation with the author (2 October 2009).

14   Leonard Manasseh, 'Low Pitched Revival', *RIBA Journal*, February 1980, p41.

15   Leonard Manasseh, 'A House at Sonning', *Architectural Association Journal*, January 1943, p54; AA presidential address, *Arena*, vol. 80 no. 886, November 1964, p99.

16   Manasseh described this as his first built project: Manasseh BL interviews, Tape 3 Side B.

17   The Coxes (married in 1943) and the Manassehs lived on different floors in the same building, belonging to Leo de Syllas, at 54 Southwood Road, Highgate, before moving to their new houses.

18   Undated cuttings in a Manasseh family album (private collection).

19   The house and (separately) Hardy Henrion's sculpture were listed Grade II* in 2009.

20   These have survived largely unchanged on the northern (entrance) front, but with alterations towards their gardens. A further project for a more distant family connection was a large but unbuilt house at Hamble-le-Rice in Hampshire for Peter Raymond, c.1957.

21   So Richard Lester told the author in a conversation in 1983.

22   The Behrens scheme appears in *Arena*, June 1964, p22; the photograph referred to here was reproduced to accompany the report of the presidential lecture (*Arena*, November 1964, p99), and a sketch by Manasseh based on it appeared above the contents list at the start of the June issue.

23   The builder was Nicholas Cocke, the son of Peter Cocke from Architects' Co-Partnership who was a neighbour of the Manassehs in Bacon's Lane.

24   London Metropolitan Archives (LMA), GLC/AR/BR/06/060346; *Survey of London*, vol. 42 p182.

25   Manasseh was doubtful about the scheme at first, but later admitted to Huddleston that it was a success. The client was pleased too, and went on to commission Huddleston to design, from the partnership's office, a private house called Giffords at Hadlow Down in East Sussex. Author's conversations with Robert Huddleston, 12/15 March 2010.

26   The plans have survived in Canterbury City Council Archives, ES/6/63/585A.

27   King's College Cambridge Archive Centre: plans, GRA/921; estates committee minutes 25 April 1969, v (a).

28   A front extension was added in 1986 and a rear one in 1988.

29   See Rob and Hugh Dunsterville, *Freik – the private life of the Freikaiserwagen*, Shelsley Walsh, Midland Automobile Club, 2008.

30   See Andy Garnett's excellent obituary in the *Independent*, 27 July 2005. Fry was at the AA from 1942 to 1943, and 1946 to 1948.

31   The presidential address is reproduced in *Arena*, vol. 80 no. 886, November 1964, pp95–100. There is a short reference to this in its context in Lionel

Esher, *A Broken Wave*, London, Allen Lane, 1981, p66.

32 *Arena*, November 1964, p101.

33 For example, in a letter to *Arena* from Michael Glickman, December 1964, pp147–8.

34 *Architectural Review*, November 1956, p336.

35 ibid., pp335–6.

36 'Eye Rattlers', from an unknown newspaper, in an undated clipping in a Manasseh family album (private collection).

37 According to H. T. Cadbury-Brown, Hugh Casson may have recommended the partnership for this project (source: Elain Harwood).

38 Manasseh BL interviews, Tape 1 Side A.

39 See London Metropolitan Archives, GLC/AR/BR/13/154133, for building regulation drawings.

40 The comparison was made later, indirectly, in an article by C. Fleetwood-Walker, 'Is Your Pyramid Really Necessary', *Listener*, 28 February 1963, pp369–70. The writer said he had 'counted at least fifteen Egyptian-type pyramids in a casual glance through last year's architectural magazines'. The author's thanks to David Etherton for drawing his attention to this.

41 Manasseh said that the cutting and mitring of the arrises, of which he was proud, was inspired by a similar detail on a roof designed by Edward Maufe, presumably that at St Columba's Church of Scotland in Pont Street, London (1950–4). Manasseh BL interviews, Tape 6 Side B.

42 Jack Whitehead: see List of Works for details.

43 The original receptionist's desk in the entrance lobby had a projecting concrete embrasure decorated with quatrefoils, a Dalwood trademark.

44 *Guardian*, 1 July 1960.

45 Quoted by Elain Harwood, English Heritage research report, 1997.

3   Piano Nobile

The Rutherford School was a critical success, and furthermore it was completed early and below budget. The reputation of the partnership was thus established, and before long it was growing so fast that staff became too numerous for their offices in Bedford Street, directly above those of the magazine *The Lady*. In 1962, they took two floors above Jeremy Fry's own premises at 26 Charlotte Street, a minute's walk across Tottenham Court Road from the AA. When the number of people working for the partnership neared 25, extra rooms had to be rented – and three architects found themselves in a little room off Rathbone Passage. Several young architects and trainees from the Commonwealth worked for the partnership on and off, contributing to the lively atmosphere. Some organisation was needed, and this was provided by an office manager – Manasseh's friend Roger Cunliffe, who had arrived back from a spell in the office of Harry Weese in Chicago. Cunliffe's wife Clemency had been the partnership's secretary at the time when he had been project architect for Robert Matthew Johnson-Marshall's Commonwealth Institute in Kensington in the late 1950s.[1] Manasseh and Cunliffe wrote a book together for Batsford entitled *Office Buildings*, dedicated 'by one of the co-authors to the other (and his wife) who did most of the work'. However, the two big projects that followed directly on from Rutherford School were for the public sector.

Furzedown Teachers' Training College

The first and larger of these consisted of various extensions to Furzedown Teachers' Training College at Tooting, in south London. This set of buildings was unusual for the practice, and aroused considerable professional interest at the time. The college was located in the grounds of a plain late Georgian house, a trapezoidal site of some three hectares (7.45 acres). A number of neo-classical buildings, very institutional in appearance, had been built along the north and south sides of the grounds in the early 20th century. The college belonged to the LCC which, at the beginning of the 1960s, wanted to expand the number of students on the site very rapidly from 450 to 600, and to provide community facilities and laboratories as well as accommodation. The large number of bedsits required encouraged the architects to build high, but not too high: a block of up to 30.48 metres (100 feet) could be approved without a planning inquiry. Thus an 11-storey tower formed the centrepiece of the design, providing 160 of the required rooms and additional wardens' accommodation. A further 84 students were to be housed in a pair of linked four-storey blocks. The project included a common room,

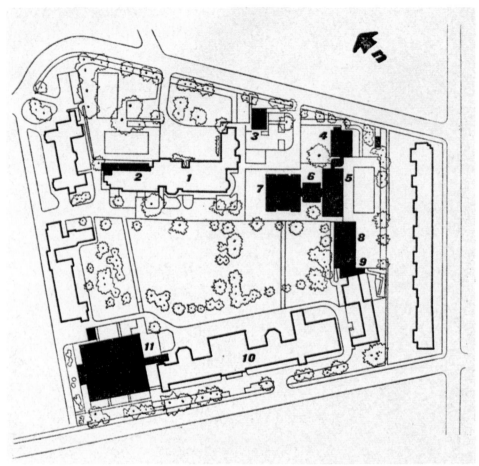

Key
1   Furzedown House
2   New music room
3   Principal's house

4,5 Four-storey residential
    blocks
6   Common room
7   Tower block

8   Science block
9   Schoolkeeper's house
10 Existing college building
11 Communal block

a large dining hall and kitchen, an assembly hall, a science block, and music practice rooms. The college principal and the school-keeper (that is, the janitor or porter) were to have new houses.

The size of the grounds, the different functions of the new structures, and the dispersal of the potential building sites around the edge of the site in order to maintain a reasonable central garden led to a remarkable decision on the part of the architects. In a move that does not seem to have been imitated in any of their other large projects, each major building would have a distinctly different appearance, with Baker

above **Furzedown College, Tooting, London: the site plan.**

as principal designer for all but one of them. The tower block needed to be built in time for the arrival of students in September 1963, about three years from the date of the architects' commission, and so the decision was taken to build it from structural pre-cast units, each of which could form the external wall of a student bedroom. These units were designed with a boldly projecting window frame to add variety and shadow to the walls, and with a projecting lower edge which sat on and in front of the floor slab below. This projection also mastered the top of the wall panel beneath, creating a kind of concrete 'shiplap' which was intended to improve the thermal insulation of the slab.[2] The units were further fixed to the slab with steel props hidden within the walls that divided the bedsits. The casting of the units was carried out on site by the Modular Concrete Company Ltd, and the procedure and the rapid speed with which it was carried out – only five months – were sufficiently unusual to be discussed in detail in the technical press.

The building is remarkable also because its aesthetics are unique in the partnership's oeuvre and because it contrasts so strongly with the more typical character of the rest of the new buildings on the Furzedown site. At first it seems that the tower has a bluntness that suggests contemporary Brutalism; its appearance undoubtedly reflects its construction method in the way that Manasseh at least had always believed it should,

above **Structural cladding panels on the Furzedown tower, photographed in 2010.**

in line with the true aesthetic of Brutalism. If a brick building should 'speak' of bricks, as Manasseh's certainly do, then a pre-cast concrete assembly should be equally honest. It was claimed at the time that the deep projections in the cladding panels, as well as giving 'great textural interest' (and, less convincingly, reducing vertigo on the part of the residents), would be enhanced by weathering. Once one has got over the shock of the form of the building as a whole, this indeed proves to be the case. The building is in fact not badly stained, and the darkening that has occurred in places has emphasised the structural idea. The principal problem with the building's appearance today is that its rear, north-eastern, side, with its corridor windows and modest fire escape doors, has become its most prominent elevation because of a subdivision of the college site. The frames of the recent windows are also considerably less subtle than the original ones. The tower's ground-floor lobby was decorated internally with patterns sunk into the concrete walls. These were decorated soon after construction with mirror-glass mosaic by the partnership's staff, who came in over a weekend to do it.[3]

The location of the tower was planned with considerably delicacy. From the south-west, it provides an effective foil for the Georgian Furzedown House; when seen from within the house, it stands at the centre of the other residences and the laboratory block. This latter group was faced in Leicester grey bricks, in imitation of English bond. The pair of residential buildings, linked by a curved staircase tower, have wide windows for their study-bedrooms and vertical slits to indicate utility areas and corridors. The

above **The science block, photographed in 2010.**

above top The Principal's house: the only part of the scheme to have been demolished.
above The dining and assembly hall.

narrow windows continue irregularly along the whole of the north-west front of the science block to indicate that this is the service side of the building. The two-storey Principal's house, designed by Manasseh, stood across a service court from the tower to the north. Unlike the other low buildings, however, its brick walls were pierced with a variety of windows, every one different. Above it rose an asymmetrical, largely glazed butterfly roof and an artfully placed chimney. It is the only significant part of the original scheme to have been completely demolished, although parts of the ground-floor links that connected the tower with its new neighbours were remodelled and extended when a section of the complex became halls of residence for the University of the Arts.

Finally, at the westernmost corner of the site, stood Baker's dining and assembly hall block – perhaps the most overtly Corbusian, in concept and in practice, of all of the partnership's executed buildings. It is still possible to see how the structure was conceived as a temple on a podium, crisply detailed as a tall glass box set between brick piers that support a concrete cornice above a long narrow continuous clerestory. Apse-like curved projections housing staircases rise from its eastern side. The plan of the building aims at a kind of liturgical simplicity. The 'temple' is the assembly hall: nothing more than a tall, bright, undivided room articulated by the piers and by the deep beams that link them below the ceiling. Beneath this is the dining hall, and, below the podium, the kitchen, cloakroom, common rooms and ancillary areas. The purpose of the apse-like stairs was to link the assembly hall stage with future changing rooms below. The glazed two-storey link block that forms part of the complex on its eastern side originally housed an art gallery on its upper floor, and provided a ceremonial route directly into the assembly hall from the stairs of the old college. Its emphatic broad concrete bands and stair strings demonstrate the structural system of the building. The sculptural effect was further enhanced by the window treatments on the lowest floor of the main structure: these were merely narrow vertical slots between the piers, or were divided up with closely spaced deep timber mullions that have survived. This building was superbly photographed both by Colin Westwood for the *Architect & Building News* and by H. de Burgh Galwey for the *Architectural Review*, creating some of the most memorable published images associated with the partnership.

Gilbert Murray Hall

The second of the two major educational projects that were probably launched by the Rutherford School was initiated in January 1962, when the Registrar of the University of Leicester wrote to Manasseh to ask him whether he wished to be considered for appointment as architect for a new hall of residence. This came on the advice of Sir Leslie Martin, Manasseh's ally, who was then consultant to the university.[4] Manasseh immediately took the train up to Leicester to present examples of his work, and the following day the Registrar wrote to the headmaster at Rutherford to say that members of its buildings committee would like to see his school.[5]

above top Gilbert Murray Hall, University of Leicester: the dining block.
above left Looking down the central lawn, from the dining block.
above right Residential block with upper-floor sub-warden's flat (above right).

Gilbert Murray Hall, as the Leicester residences eventually became known, was located in an area of smart Edwardian villas between the main university site near the city centre and Oadby to the south-east. At the time, the university was developing this as a residential village for students. The site on Manor Road included a large villa, which was retained in the partnership's plan; its ground floor provided a formal route through to a new dining hall and kitchen across a lawn to the south. Doors on the far side of this hall led towards a long open garden, bounded on each side by a terrace of student rooms. At the northern end of one of them there was a laundry building with a tall chimney. To the east of this main vista there was a third set of terraces, and a low warden's lodge at the north-east corner of the site completed the scheme.

The authors of the Leicestershire *Buildings of England Guide* see the complex as owing something to Dudok. The stepped massing of the brick terraces, and in particular of the laundry with its tall chimney, owes something to Dutch constructionism but to de Klerk and Kramer rather than Dudok. However, Gilbert Murray Hall has other qualities too, including an original plan. Within each block of about 30 rooms, a steep open stair originally rose up through the communal kitchens to the top-floor sub-wardens' flats with their large balconies. The stair balustrades were the partnership's typical type, with a circular handrail and no banisters, so anyone rising up through the building really did

above **Gilbert Murray Hall: the central lawn, with the laundry block at the far right-hand side.**

feel as if they were in the middle of all the activity going on around them. The square hall with its canted corners also followed what was becoming Manasseh's characteristic solution for this type: a tall, almost flat roof sat over a continuous narrow clerestory, and a 45-degree pitched roof brought this down to the walls, with triangular windows bridging the spaces between them. Working drawings for the scheme were done by Michael Hopkins, then a recent AA graduate.[6]

The areas between the buildings were important too. The central garden is a lawn, but the south and east sides of the complex are glimpsed through trees. An external roofed walkway, with narrow steel columns, originally ran along the site between the hall and the front of the old house in order to 'manage' the views of the complex on arrival. In fact, overall the atmosphere of the site, which incorporated two mature gardens, is more Nordic than Dutch. An interesting comparison can be drawn with the contemporary Stamford Hall designed by Denys Lasdun on a site close by to the west. This takes the form of a rigid north–south spine of three-storey residences over 130 metres (425 feet) long with abutting, boldly roofed structures housing communal areas towards one end – a building that is intended to reveal itself in one single breathtaking moment.[7]

Housing in the New Towns

It was not a fact much advertised by the partnership, but substantial commissions from the Royal Air Force for new housing supported the office for some time during the years of their expansion. However, other commissions, mainly for four large estates in and around London, provided opportunities for original work during the period when professional and critical interest in the development of new forms of housing was probably at its peak.

Harlow was one of the first designated new towns to be established following the passing of the New Towns Act of 1946. The purpose of the Act was to reduce the population of London by over one million from its pre-war total through the creation of publicly planned and managed towns beyond the green belt, broadly along the lines of the ideas of the Garden City Movement. However, Harlow was different from the other towns of the period, for example Stevenage, in that it retained the same architect consultant, Frederick Gibberd, for the whole of the existence of its new town corporation. Gibberd, one of Manasseh's supporters from AA days, himself presided over the designs for the first areas of housing to be built in the town – and brought in many of his friends and former students. Much of the housing was in the Scandinavian style familiar from the Lansbury Estate at the 'Live Architecture' exhibition at Poplar.

In spite of these unpretentious beginnings, and the architect's insistence on low rise housing divided by the prominent green 'wedges' that make much of it invisible from the roads, Harlow contains a great deal of experimental housing, including equally original localisedtraffic and pedestrian schemes. Such was the esteem that Gibberd was held in that his personal recommendations for the appointments of architect – his 'impresario'

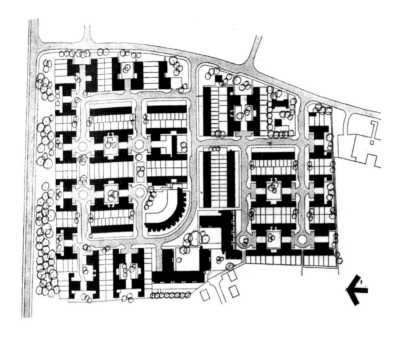

role, as the *Architectural Review* put it – seem to have been widely supported by the corporation even when others protested.[8] In 1963, the partnership was thus appointed to design an estate for rent near the south-west boundary of the town, referred to in the town's master plan as Area 84. It was just under eight hectares (19.33 acres) in size and was located in the Kingswood area, between Southern Way and Ployters Road.[9]

The dimensions of the site, which was eventually named Brockles Mead, and the requirement to provide a relatively dense mix of 425 housing units, each with its own garage, made it difficult for the architects to separate vehicular traffic from walkways in the Radburn-type layout that was generally favoured at the time. The partnership thus decided to try the exact opposite. Their idea was that car circulation would be integrated as closely as possible to the pedestrian one. Manasseh in fact claimed that children would be more likely to want to play out in the garage courts, where a father might be cleaning a car, than on a landscaped green where nothing was going on.[10] The idea was thus a harbinger of the Dutch concept of the *woonerf*, the integrated street where pedestrians have priority over motor vehicles, which was not yet a feature of English suburban planning.

Much of the Brockles Mead scheme was thus taken up with stock-brick courtyard blocks in which a children's play area at the centre of a cluster was bounded on two sides by house entrances and on the other two by garage courts. Around the edges of these, and beyond private gardens, were terraces of houses. At the highest point on

above **Brockles Mead, Harlow New Town, Essex: site plan.**

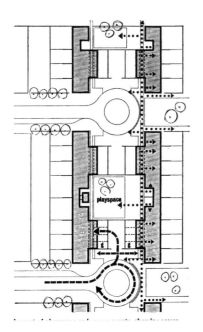

the site, at the centre of the western side, there was a quadrant of flats that faced two
L-shaped maisonette blocks. These large blocks were planned to suit a clump of fully
grown trees ('like a sacred grove', said Manasseh), but the latter were cut down by the
contractor.[11] The project was illustrated with detailed plans and two fine drawings
by the partnership, a perspective of the characteristic garage courts and a section
through one of the L-shaped blocks, in the *Architectural Review*. Work started on site in
November 1965, and was complete by May 1968.

The way that vehicle traffic is integrated into the pedestrian walkways undoubtedly
has disadvantages: particularly unfortunate is the way in which the main distributor
road, leading from Ployters Road to the quadrant of flats, is lined to the south with a
row of garages. Not only is it impossible to control the appearance of the doors, but
also the continuous driveways and entry paths prevent any planting along the route. It
was perhaps also wishful thinking to assume that a car would slow down enough to be
truly safe on entering a long cul-de-sac. On the other hand, however, the symmetrical
and stepped grouping of the buildings and courts around the play areas produced a
comparatively rich townscape in which no space seems wasted or orphaned. The incorporation of the garages and the walls of the play areas into the overall architecture
of the courtyard blocks resulted in a high level of homogeneity which is enlivened by
the busy sawtooth patterns of the gables. The ensemble illustrates Manasseh's almost

above left **Detail of typical parking and play areas.**
above right **The block of large flats at the western edge of the site.**

contemporary remark, in his 1964 AA presidential address, that 'the planning of environment is and always has been a function of Total Architecture'. The rebuilding of the roofs of the flats in the long orthogonal blocks has disrupted their sculptural character, but in general the scheme remains much as it was originally designed.

above top **Typical housing cluster.**
above **The quadrant of flats towards the western edge of the site.**

above top Brockles Mead in 2010: a view towards one of the courtyard blocks showing the sawtooth gables.
above Brockles Mead in 2010.

The Steeplehall Estate at Basildon New Town, commissioned soon after the
Harlow one, was more conventional in its overall approach: it was designed to a lower
density than Brockles Mead and it also achieved more of a separation between roads
and paths. It was a much larger scheme, with 739 units occupying a site of about 16
hectares (39.53 acres) in an important position close to the centre of Pitsea, Basildon's
eastern hub.[12] Hopkins worked on the master plan, and the overall approach was
considerably more formal than at Harlow. An almost identical cluster of mixed units
was repeated several times across the site – four-and-a-half times along the northern
perimeter, and one-and-a-half times on the southern side – leaving a large open
space in the middle that formed part of a continuous green area between estates.
The brilliant stroke here was that these clusters were slightly staggered so as to
ensure that the gable ends of one set of maisonette blocks appeared neatly at the
centre of the east–west axial views from the roadways and paths of the neighbouring
cluster, a device perfectly suited to the practice's style. At the same time, pathways
ran uninterrupted along grand symmetrical vistas from north to south, passing
through openings in the low terraces of houses towards the central park. Most of
the housing is in the form of two-storey terraced units. At the park end of the
northern clusters, these terminate in box-like forms that provide an upper terrace,
edged by a tall parapet, for the residents, but which give the impression of a row
of fortifications to passers-by. The maisonette blocks all run east–west; along the

above **The Steeplehall Estate, Basildon New Town, Essex, in 2010: one of the axial-block gables.**

The Steeplehall Estate soon after completion.

northern boundary on Wickford Avenue these resemble ships, with receding prows at either end. The tall blocks at the centres of the clusters are the ones that most exploit the staggering of the axis, emphasised by the expressionistic modelling of their brick balustrades and their clerestoried gables. The estate was completed, like Brockles Mead, in 1968. Just before this, the practice completed a separate estate of 24 old people's houses in Parkhurst Road nearby, for which they won an award.[13]

The separation of traffic from the access paths has been somewhat compromised by the fact that the latter now have wide asphalted surfaces that themselves resemble roads. Without the density of Brockles Mead, the homogeneous brickwork no longer quite holds the scheme together. Landscaping has been unimaginative, and the original porches that were in the form of flat-roofed timber cabins with horizontal slit windows were nearly all replaced in the late 1980s by a variety of brick constructions with pitched roofs, so the overall geometry of the terraces has lost its clarity. Furthermore, the arrival of individualised plastic windows with coarse mullions has, as so often, taken its toll. If the temple-like form of the Furzedown assembly hall, high on its splendid podium, was Leonard Manasseh's Chandigarh, it is hard to escape the conclusion that Steeplehall has become his Pessac.[14]

London housing

At the same time that Brockles Mead and Steeplehall were under way in the new towns, the partnership worked on two estates in London. Further work on these projects continued well into the 1970s. Both were distinct from their suburban schemes, and both remarkable in the way that they contrasted with much accepted architectural practice at the time by being emphatically vertical in their proportions. Equally remarkable was the original way in which they appeared to borrow from traditional terraced housing forms without any trace of the vernacular pastiche so despised by Manasseh.

The first and more conventional project was that around Dodson Street in Waterloo, the greater part of which was designed for the London County Council in 1962 with Baker in charge and John Roberts as designer and project architect. The scheme for the site – about three-quarters of a hectare (1.85 acres) between Dodson Street, Gerridge Street and Westminster Bridge Road – was for 96 units, almost entirely maisonettes but also with five single-family houses and a two-storey block for old people's one-room flats.[15] In the executed plan, the maisonettes were arranged into three six-storey blocks facing south-west and south-east across two sides of a large open playground. The two- and three-bedroom maisonettes had split-level scissor sections, with rooms at the back of the block separated from those at the front by half a floor. Thus in their general overall form the blocks were conventional, but the verticality of their detailing makes them stand out. This was achieved through several devices, all relying on the use of bold red brickwork: the tall chimneys that coincided with the party walls between flats, the almost uninterrupted stair towers separated by shadow gaps from the main bulk of the

blocks, and the sculptural modelling of the narrow end elevations. The ground-floor flats in these blocks have pitched-roof extensions, not unlike the kitchen extensions of much older London houses but with large windows occupying the side walls. The brickwork is made to look like Flemish garden wall bond, and the *in situ* concrete string above the ground floor is cast with a delicate brickwork pattern.

The partnership's design came a year after Darbourne & Darke's widely publicised scheme for the Lillington Gardens Estate in Pimlico and shares its vibrant red brick and its split-level plans, but Dodson Estate's verticality is its own. The five houses with their ridge clerestory windows were positioned at 45 degrees to the pavement in a staggered row along Westminster Bridge Road, suggesting that their location was as much to do with creating a dramatic view of the estate from the main route past it as anything else; the old people's blocks in Dodson Street itself are staid, almost Festival-like, by comparison. In 1966, a further maisonette block, Guthrie Court, was added on Gerridge Street parallel to a previous block and following the same design.

The partnership returned to the estate at the end of the 1970s, when they added a further 63 units in three different blocks at the northern apex of the site in a style that relates more closely to those at their remarkable estate at Hoxton that was by then

above left **The Dodson Street Estate, Waterloo, London, photographed when new from Westminster Bridge Road.**
above right **The Dodson Street Estate in 2010.**

complete. Here the office trademark, the sawtooth pattern, is achieved through the plans rather than the elevations. The front elevation is dominated by the emphatic lines of the brick balcony-access 'corridor' balustrades that run parallel to Waterloo Road, but the external walls of the flats behind them are arranged in a zigzag. The form is more clearly expressed on the rear elevation, where, in contrast, the appearance of the walls again suggests terraced houses. All the buildings on the estate are well maintained, even if the fenestration has lost its original delicacy, and the landscaping has been kept up much as the architects originally intended it.

Of all the partnership's large housing schemes, the Hoxton one, properly called the Arden Estate extension, is the most original and memorable. The existing estate was located just north of Hoxton Square near Shoreditch, and comprised LCC blocks from different periods and in different styles – mainly in brick with access balconies. Here the partnership, led this time by Manasseh, designed 115 dwellings on a narrow

above **The Arden Estate extension, Hoxton, London: a view of the Hoxton Street link block.**

site formerly occupied by terraced houses between the estate's existing buildings. The work was commissioned in 1967 and approved by the GLC Housing Department the following year. For this project, the engineers, unusually for the partnership it appears, were Ove Arup – one department of which worked in the same building as the partnership itself.[16] The estate was completed in 1972, when the small square site of the Hoxton Café that had survived the rebuilding all around it was acquired and redeveloped as part of the overall scheme.

The housing was mostly accommodated in six blocks of four-storey maisonettes, three on either side of a lane called Myrtle Walk which ran from east to west. In addition, there was a tower linking two of the southern blocks which lay at right angles to each other, and, eventually, a further tower on the Hoxton Café site. In spite of the fact that these were again balcony-access flats, the division of the buildings into vertical units was even more vigorous than at Dodson Street. In the two linked blocks, narrow red-brick piers at regular intervals rise up from the pavement to support rear-extension-type brick outhouses (in fact housing bedrooms) high up in the air; when seen at an angle from the street, the buildings divide into broad vertical stripes of bright and dark red. On the Crondall Street blocks, the piers terminate in fins – imitating party-wall divisions – and further upward thrust is given by the tiled refuse chutes. Necessary horizontal bands, for example the outside edges of the access-balcony slabs, are faced

above left **Typical access balconies and top-floor bedrooms along Hoxton Street.**
above right **Myrtle Walk. The rooftop extension is by Patrick Lynch Associates, 2005.**

in a browner brick and the balustrades are made of glass in order to avoid distracting attention from the piers.

The blocks create lively and unexpected vistas, especially as they unfurl the length of Hoxton Street. The partnership had generally tried to punch windows into the brick walls of domestic or residential buildings in the form of simple geometric shapes – squares or slits – and here they perfected the detail. Maybe for this reason the projecting extensions at top-floor level, sitting up on their stilts, have with their single sharp 'eye' something of an anthropomorphic quality to them; perhaps they are a phalanx of long-legged space-age moonwalkers. The terraces above ground level on the Myrtle Walk side of the long east–west blocks are divided by curved brick wall enclosures; their use is unexplained, but they set up unexpected views when looking towards the two towers. It is remarkable too that the south elevations of the blocks, particularly the southern ones, mimic terraced houses in other ways: they have large full-height windows on the first floor, for example, which are protected by glass balustrades placed on the wall plane. They have in other words a *piano nobile*, which the stacked-maisonette plan does not necessarily suggest. They also have 'attics', very different from the rigidly horizontal roofline of every earlier block on the Arden Estate. The elevations of the two tower buildings are original too: the earlier one that links the maisonette blocks is again frankly Dudokian; the Hoxton Café one, with its curious cascading conservatory roof and irregular fenestration, is a remarkable piece of sculpture. Its recent upward glazed extension by Patrick Lynch Architects enhances it, even if it softens its former stunted oddness. The unusual and haunting profiles of the buildings certainly put one in mind of some of Manasseh's expectant, moonlit scenes.

At Rathbone Street

The partnership enjoyed its second busy period in the early 1970s as the Hoxton scheme was under way. Since 1965, its London offices had occupied most of two upper floors at 13 Rathbone Street, above the Race Furniture showroom. The area was still relatively seedy; it was mainly populated by commercial artists and the building itself still had something of the quality of a warehouse, complete with an unused goods lift. The practice was presided over by Rhoda Kelly, the partnership's long-serving office manager who also acted as Manasseh's and Baker's private secretary. Unlike the partners, she had a keen business sense and was generally credited with keeping both architects and clients on their toes. All who worked there agree that the atmosphere was unfailingly congenial; there were, for example, memorable Christmas parties. The partners often went out for Charlotte Street lunches, usually in Bertorelli's. The other architects in the office patronised a working-men's café nearby, or the tiny Newman Arms pub.[17]

Roger W. Morgan, who joined the office in August 1973 on completing his diploma at Manchester University, recalled this period as the happiest of his life. He kept a detailed account of his time there, as well as a plan which records where everyone sat.

There were then 18 people in the office. Leonard Manasseh and Ian Baker occupied a large room at the front, although in practice Manasseh spent much time away in connection with his increasing activities at the RIBA and the Royal Academy, and in general representing the office to clients and public bodies. Behind their room sat the receptionist (two, when business was at its peak) and a conference room. Kelly had a small office at the back, and the rest of the space on that floor was divided into two with double-elephant drawing boards on long wooden tables; Morgan recalls that dust sheets were placed over them before going home at night. On the floor above sat Geoffrey Scarsbrook, by now a partner, with his own team. John Thake, whose initials can be seen on many of the partnership's working drawings, also sat upstairs in a corner of his own. He had begun a career in architecture through traditional pupillage, and was an extremely capable technician. On leaving the office in 1973 he qualified as an architect, eventually becoming managing director of the international practice Aukett. Many other architects and students came and went. Some, like John Roberts, a former employee of Ernö Goldfinger and an associate of the partnership who had worked on Garth Castle, reappeared several times over a long period; at one point he was working for Peter Moro in the same building. Roberts, a perfectionist, was the practice's third designer for a period. Following Roger Cunliffe's reforms, the working practices of the office were further modernised for the Beaulieu project when Christopher Hulls

above **Ian Baker at work in the partners' room at 13 Rathbone Street, 1973.**

joined; he came from working on the Brunswick Centre for Patrick Hodgkinson, and introduced the method of dividing up work into design packages.

The project teams had distinct identities, which to some extent expressed themselves in the type of work they specialised in. Bryan Field had worked with Manasseh and Baker since the early-1950s. In that decade he had been the project architect for a number of small office buildings, most of them attached to existing works premises, and in the early 1960s he worked continuously on the RAF housing schemes. The largest of the office projects for which he had been job architect was the building at David Fry's Frenchay works at Kingswood, under Baker. A smaller example was for the perfumery department of Lautier Fils Ltd, a little building adjacent to the company's existing works at Power Road, off Chiswick High Road in west London, which survived into the 2000s. It was a two-storey red-brick building with continuous horizontal glazing along the street front and a wooden brise-soleil at cornice level. Field generally worked on the public-housing projects for which Baker was the partner in charge, often together with Thake. He was seen by the staff as a pragmatist who got things done; they remember him also for his gentle and forgiving nature.[18]

A member of the Open Brethren, Field was responsible for the only religious buildings undertaken by the practice. In the early to mid-1960s he designed a church and classrooms in Greenford in Middlesex, followed by the street-front extension to the gospel hall at Canbury Park, Kingston, which was completed in 1974. Field was also the job architect for an entirely new hall on a site in Stracey Road, Harlesden, in north-west London. This was a low single-storey building of Forticrete blocks with glazed ends to the north and south topped with a small glazed pyramid, in 'house style',

above **Christopher Press (left) and Geoffrey Scarsbrook celebrating the partnership's 25th anniversary in 1975 at Freshford.**

over the centre of the main part of its roof.[19] When originally built, this economical structure was dominated by its backdrop: the pre-cast concrete 14-storey Mordaunt House, part of the Stonebridge Estate, immediately to its west. The environment today is somewhat different: Mordaunt House has gone, and to the south of the hall, which is now a Christian centre on the edge of a large empty space, a row of Manassehesque terraced houses with steep monopitch gable ends has recently been erected.

By the early 1970s, Scarsbrook had also been with the partners for more than a decade. At the beginning he had worked on the office block at Rotork, but by and large he concentrated on one-off projects, including restaurant designs and interior remodelling work, that required a high level of detailing. One of these was the museum for the 'Exhibition of the Queen's Presents and Royal Carriages' that he created out of and around the stable yard between the Royal Mews and St Alban's Street in Windsor, just to the south of the castle precincts. The gallery was established following a fire in 1975. Commissioned by the Property Services Agency (PSA) of the Department of the Environment, it was to occupy a red-brick stable block that opened on to the street, the yard itself and some rooms on the ground floor of Burford House, a castellated building on the mews side that had possibly originally been designed by George III but which had been remodelled by Jeffry Wyatville at the beginning of Victoria's reign as a residence for castle staff.[20] The principal element of the scheme was a glazed pavilion that occupied almost all of the yard, retaining the original cobbled street and pavement as a floor. This was linked by arches and ramps through to the roadside stables, which were themselves converted into a reception area, a small shop and an exhibition gallery. A further gallery and WCs were located within Burford House, and the practice

above **Shrewsbury Gospel Hall in Harlesden, London. It has lasted longer than the other buildings seen here.**

designed the glass exhibition cabinets which were used throughout. The highlight of the design was undoubtedly the glazed court, where five Ascot landaus sat in illuminated splendour, their fine black wheels and spokes beautifully complemented by the minimal, elegant glazing bars of the building – a memorable interpretation of Manasseh's idea of an efficient construction employing the visual language of a machine. He drew a series of perspectives of the project, showing colourful elongated figures making their way through the rooms, which the Association of Consultant Architects presented to Queen Elizabeth II to mark her Silver Jubilee in 1977.[21] The museum was completed that year and remained in use until 1995 when the complex became the castle's education centre. The buildings remain, without any of their fittings, but the landaus and the rest of the carriages are now housed at Buckingham Palace.

Scarsbrook's job architect was John Birkett-Smith, who had begun primarily as an assistant to the partnership's planning consultant, Elizabeth Chesterton, and eventually became a qualified planner but who by the mid-1970s was spending about half of his time with the architectural side of the practice. Apart from the remodelling of a branch of the National Westminster Bank in Finchley, Windsor was his first project in charge.[22] However, Scarsbrook generally collaborated with the Swiss-born architect Alex Billeter, with whom he forged a strong bond. Billeter had first worked for the partnership in

above Leonard Manasseh's view of the Windsor Royal Mews Museum, painted for Queen Elizabeth II in 1977.

1967–8 as a student, and then, following a stay in the United States, returned in 1971 for a further nine years. He had studied at the Eidgenössische Technische Hochschule (ETH) in Zurich. Billeter first came to the practice on the recommendation of a college friend, Alex Bloch – later an important Jerusalem architect – who had himself done a year's training at the practice the year beforehand.[23] Manasseh apparently trusted the ETH to provide its students with a better grounding in construction details than British schools of architecture did – and for his part Billeter was amazed, when he first went on a site visit with his new employers, to find that British local authorities were still building balcony-access flats. In addition to this type of work, he drew perspectives which were embellished by the firm's partners for display or publication. He also designed an extension to the Lighthouse, the small bungalow at Sandwich. At Hedingham County Secondary School in Essex, he designed a building to complement an earlier one by Scarsbrook.

In addition to the London premises the practice maintained a presence near Bath, housed in austere splendour in a former brewery building at Freshford, about ten minutes' drive away from the city to the south-east. The office was managed by Christopher Press, another AA graduate, who opened it in 1967 after four years with the partnership; he became a partner himself in 1973. From Freshford, he designed and ran a number of the larger housing projects including the Hunters Moon Estate near Dartington, flats in Redcross Street in central Bristol and a development of 365 houses north of the Eastfield Road in the north of the city. He also worked on projects such as Rotork and the Curtis house at Lower Radley, and several of the schemes described in the next chapter – including Torr and the hotel at Buckler's Hard near Beaulieu.

The Freshford brewery was a large eighteenth-century building at the centre of the village. With its crisp gables and tall chimneys, it looked rather as if it might have been designed by Manasseh himself. An attached cottage house at the northern end of the building provided modest overnight accommodation for visitors from London, but the greater part consisted of one enormous room, over 15 metres (50 feet) long, scarcely refurbished from its original use and very sparsely furnished. About five people at most were based there at any one time, and at the start Press lived in Avondale, the former brewmaster's house that formed part of the complex. Unlike the London office, it was extremely quiet. Richard Partridge, son of Manasseh's friend John Partridge, worked there during his 'year out' in 1977 (not long after another student, Richard Feilden, had left the office) and remembers that no one, least of all Press, said a word most of the time. Visits from London partners or staff were rare. Partridge's impression is confirmed by others who worked there. It was this building that was eventually converted, by Press, into a remarkable home for Jeremy Fry in 1983–4.

From the mid-1960s onwards, it was Baker who produced most of the presentation drawings that were issued by the office, including Royal Academy Summer Exhibition work. Several of those who worked closely with him at that time saw his ability to solve a design problem and to work out the details of it as being close to genius. Given the

above top **Willis Block, Hedingham County Secondary School, Essex.**
above Freshford Brewery.

fact that any one of the four partners, and sometimes a job architect, took responsibility for the design of a project it might at first seem surprising that all of the buildings have so consistent an appearance. However, in practice all the designers worked from the same palette. Manasseh and Baker from the first devised a series of elements that repeat themselves across the work of the practice as a whole, and their hallmarks are echoed on a large and small scale wherever one looks: Manasseh's glazed or tiled pyramids, his window walls with their fine black mullions and minimal eaves, and his assertive gables such as that on his own house and those that characterise his paintings; and Baker's bold geometrical masonry forms, his grand symmetry and rhythms, and his careful pattern-making. It seems likely that, for example in the case of buildings designed by Field, they made interventions to their job architect's original design sketches in order to maintain the consistency of the language. Both partners were strong person- alities, and the staff were to some extent in awe of them. Thake remembers Baker and Manasseh holding 'crits', in the manner of those at architecture schools, to review employees' designs. Manasseh, according to both David Etherton and Donald Meyer, recalling their time in the office in the early 1960s, always had the last word in design. The long glazed wall of the Frenchay offices shares a common language with the small elegant glass exhibition cases at Windsor. Tall narrow windows punched into the brickwork, and the long clerestory ones, unite the design of the houses from Bristol to Beaulieu and Basildon.

above **The brewery at Freshford after conversion into offices for the partnership.**

The Bath debacle

There was one project which Manasseh undoubtedly designed himself – consciously trying to create a heroic, temple-like building – that he was cruelly prevented from realising. This was his project for the law courts in Bath, which he personally designed and in which he invested a great deal of energy. He saw it, perhaps, not only as his counterpart to the courts designed by Baker in King's Lynn but also as his single great project, as the National Motor Museum (see next chapter) had been for his partner.

In 1958 the architect for the city of Bath, Dr Howard Stutchbury, was asked to design a new courthouse for the city. A traffic scheme by Colin Buchanan, commissioned in 1963, provided a site for it by recommending demolition of Georgian terraced housing in Walcot Street, on the northern edge of the inner-city core, and its replacement with a multi-storey car park. The roof of the car park would be at pavement level, its bulk below built into the fall of the land down to the river which bordered the site to the east. The idea was that this would provide a podium for a hotel and public building alongside a major road artery that would incorporate a tunnel. The demolition was carried out in 1969, and the car-park podium and hotel were built, but increasing public antipathy to comprehensive development in the city put a stop to the tunnel.

By 1968 even Buchanan was calling for conservation, and four years later Stutchbury's design for law courts on the podium, in a 'revamped John Wood' style, was finally rejected by the Royal Fine Art Commission (RFAC).[24] Manasseh was invited to replace Stutchbury as architect for the project. The site was a complicated one, neighboured by terraced houses and the Victorian Gothic church of St Michael with St Paul to the south and west as well as by the plain, and already widely disliked, bulk of the hotel recently erected to the north. In addition to this, the structural columns of the car park poked up through the podium, essentially dictating the overall form of any new building. Manasseh designed his building around a core of ground-floor cells, reached from below, within a ring of public areas and offices. On the floor above, the four magistrates' courtrooms sat over the cells, with a further juvenile and domestic court to the south. The public-access hall ran the length of the outer ring of the building on the street side, with interview rooms off it. The rest of the building volume was taken up with offices and the magistrates' retiring rooms, and there was to be a roof garden above. It was a straightforward, logical plan that comfortably accommodated in two floors the detailed complexities of the access arrangements within. The exterior of the building was to be clad in concrete, because Bath stone was too expensive. However, again in contrast to much new building of the time and certainly unlike the unfortunate hotel next door, the arrangement of the façades was primarily vertical; this, Manasseh said, would reflect the traditional pattern of the city's residential streets. The character of the main elevation of the building would be determined by the eight bold columns that stood in front of the main wall plane. Manasseh linked these columns with a 2 metre (6 foot)-high parapet that stretched boldly outwards and would have hidden the inevitable machinery on the roof.

As might be expected, the walls in the panels behind these columns were detailed in such a way as to emphasise their verticality. The elevations were to have very little symmetry, in spite of the temple form. Along the street front, the windows that lit the *piano nobile* – for that is what it truly was this time – were arranged as deep, broad aedicules. At the back, they were smaller and narrower; they followed the proportions of Georgian domestic windows whereas the ones at the front suggested the grand windows of Neoclassical palaces. Some of them, for example in the area of the justices' assembly room, were topped with little circular recesses – an almost Venetian effect, continued by the elegant brackets for the adjoining balcony. It is worth noting that Gio Ponti's building at Taranto Cathedral, with its not dissimilar geometrically pierced concrete walls, had recently been completed.

The public mood in the city was, however, in no state to welcome the erection of another large freestanding concrete structure, even for a site that had already been devastated. In the autumn of 1974, a new chief architect, Roy Worskett, took over from Stutchbury and had to decide what to do about the scheme. This was in the year following the publication of Adam Fergusson's *The Sack of Bath*, one of the most successful polemical cases for urban conservation.[25] As Worskett prepared to take up his position, the *Architects' Journal* published a stinging article accompanied by the partnership's own photographic montages showing a model of the building in its

above **The proposed Bath Law Courts as seen, in a montage, from New Bond Street.**

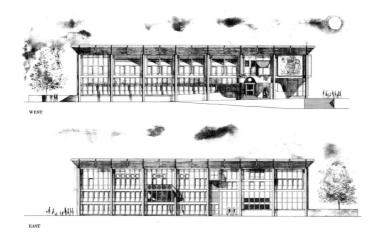

context, claiming that the design was 'fiddly, almost frenzied', and that 'what might have been acceptable in Macclesfield, is a gross irruption on the face of Bath', even if this was a situation in which no architect could win. This was, the anonymous author wrote, no place for 'hollow echoes of Chandigarh', a comment that must have been particularly wounding to the architect. Two weeks later the *Journal* published Manasseh's reply, which drew attention to the elements that his scheme shared with classical architecture. He also pointed out that the magazine had failed to publish his montage of a view from the south, which would have shown how the courts would have healed the painful gap between the old buildings of the centre and the hotel. Furthermore, he pointed out, the RFAC thought that his design 'showed promise of great distinction'. In October, however, the Bath Preservation Trust, now a rising star in local politics, greeted Worskett's appointment with a statement that the courts were 'unacceptable'. The city abandoned the scheme soon after.

It seemed on the face of it that its lobbyists and decision makers had chosen to cut off their noses to spite their faces, to leave a prominent ugly site as it was rather than

above top **The entry (above) and east elevations.**
above **The model, seen from the west.**

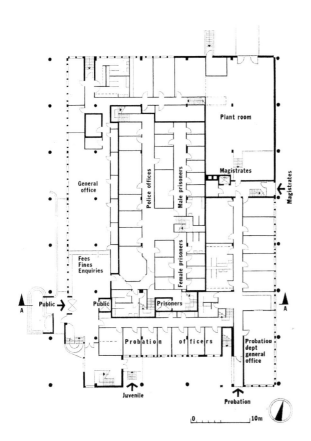

Plant room

General
office

Police offices

Male prisoners

Female prisoners

Magistrates

Magistrates

Fees
Fines
Enquiries

A ↑
Public →

Public

Prisoners

↑ A

Probation   officers

Probation
dept
general
office

Juvenile

Probation

0   10m

complete one of the most carefully worked out and detailed schemes that any architect
had devised for the city in recent times. Eventually the gap was filled by the type of
building Manasseh loathed more than any other, a supermarket clad with Neoclassical
pastiche elevations, and another architect's neo-vernacular courtroom complex went up
at a safe distance from the centre of the town.

Manasseh blamed both the *AJ* article and the new City Architect for the collapse of
a project that was particularly dear to him. During the course of his interviews with the
British Library Sound Archives in 1998, the recollection of this debacle was the single
memory that disturbed his otherwise equable temper.[26] However, Birkett-Smith points
out, the real culprit was the IRA bombing campaign of the mid-1970s. On 17 June 1974,
a nine-kilogramme (20-pound) device exploded at the Palace of Westminster, causing
extensive damage even to the thick medieval stonework of Westminster Hall; from then
on, a courthouse above a publicly accessible car park was unthinkable.

The Bath affair has an unexpected postscript. In the late 1970s, the partnership was
commissioned for a further heavy infrastructure project, a sewage pumping station and

above **Ground floor plan.**

treatment site for Wessex Water on the western side of Radipole Lake near Weymouth. Manasseh took a great deal of interest in this small project, designing a concrete pavilion cast with angled grooves and a large capital 'W', with one of his long glazed roofs running along the ridge. The site was a sensitive one, as the lake had been declared a Site of Special Scientific Interest and was also a bird sanctuary. Mike Kelly, who was the local authority deputy planning officer at the time, remembers that Manasseh deployed his diplomatic skills to the full in order to win over an openly hostile planning chairman.[27] Manasseh presented his drawing of the scheme to the Royal Academy as his diploma work following his election as an Academician in May 1979, and the project featured prominently in publicity material for the partnership. As Birkett-Smith says, he was determined to see his concrete temple built at last – even if it was only to be on a tiny scale.[28]

above Design for Radipole Lake Pumping Station, for Weymouth and Portland Borough Council, Weymouth, Devon: plan, elevation and section.

Notes

1   This description of the office and its practices at the time is based on the author's conversations with David Etherton (5 February 2010), Donald Meyer (6 February 2010), Roger Cunliffe (9 March 2010), Nigel Woolner (12 March 2010) and Robert Huddleston (12/15 March 2010).

2   Manasseh himself 'had a great deal to do with' the design of these units: Manasseh BL interviews, Tape 6 Side A.

3   Remembered by John Thake, 9 February 2010.

4   David Wilson Library, University of Leicester, EST/GMH/1–6.

5   According to Donald Meyer, there was a suggestion that more than one hall would be built.

6   Author's conversation with Sir Michael Hopkins, 10 November 2009.

7   John Thake remembers that Leonard Manasseh & Partners also designed and executed a language laboratory building on the university's main campus, but no further details have been discovered.

8   *Architectural Review*, July 1966, p37.

9   The development of Harlow, including details of the various estates, is described in Frederick Gibberd, Ben Hyde Harvey and Len White, *Harlow: the Story of a New Town*, Stevenage, Publications for Companies, 1980. Many of the partnership's layout and working drawings for the estate have survived in the collection of the Museum of Harlow, catalogued under 'Brockles Mead'.

10   ibid., pp179, 181.

11   Manasseh BL interviews, Tape 6 Side A.

12   At Steeplehall there were 46 units per hectare (19 per acre); at Brockles Mead, 54 units per hectare (22 per acre).

13   This was the Ministry of Housing Award for Good Design, South-East (northern) region (lower density public sector).

14   Le Corbusier's housing estate of 1925–8 for industrial workers at Pessac, near Bordeaux, was mutilated by its residents and for a long time the name was, for some, a byword for architectural vandalism.

15   The building regulation approval drawings are in the LMA, GLC/AR/BR/26/SO/0019/23/BA.

16   LMA: GLC/AR/BR/13/011646. The branch of Arups was at 13 Rathbone Street (see below).

17   This description of the office is based on interviews with John Birkett-Smith (16 October 2009), Alex Billeter (23 October 2009) and John Thake (9

18   This description of Field is Birkett-Smith's, and Manasseh described him as 'saintly' in his BL interviews, Tape 6 Side A. Robert Huddleston recalls that Field resisted becoming an Associate of the firm because he did not approve of differences in personal status.

19   The author's thanks to Philip Uren, of the Canbury Park congregation, who has retained copies of Field's drawings of his hall. Greenford was photographed for the Architectural Press in 1968 by Bill Toomey. The author would also like to thank David Sugden of Greenford Gospel Church for his comments on this section. The use of the blocks at Harlesden was seen as a trial run for the Beaulieu project.

20   Burford House: see Howard Colvin (ed.), *The History of the King's Works*, vol v, 1976, p340. It is unclear from this whether Wyatville also designed the red-brick stable block on St Alban's Street which was incorporated into the museum.

21   Print Room, Royal Library Windsor, RCIN 923121, 741367–70.

22   The practice seems to have designed the interior of other branches – Baker's daughter Nina remembers the colourful one decorated with a mural in Haymarket in London – but the archives of the Royal Bank of Scotland, which acquired the bank and its records, do not mention its involvement. The practice also included the Midland Bank in a 1996 summary of clients.

23   Bloch, who died in 1995, was in 1979 with David Guggenheim a founding partner of Guggenheim/Bloch, which carried out large-scale urban rehabilitation projects and various highly regarded residential schemes in the city.

24   The story is told in the *Architects Journal*, 7 August 1974 pp306–8; the anonymous writer was Peter Davey. See also the *Pevsner Architectural Guides: Bath*, by Michael Forsyth, pp46–7, 130 and 223, for a general outline of the period and descriptions of the architectural sites involved.

25   Adam Fergusson, *The Sack of Bath*, Salisbury, Russell/Bath Preservation Trust, 1973.

26   Manasseh BL interviews, Tape 7 Side A.

27   Mike Kelly's email to the author, 17 December 2009.

28   In 2009, the pumping station was due to be decorated with large murals.

4   Loggia

Sitting in her own room on the first floor of the Rathbone Street office, a consultant to the practice but not actually a partner in it, was the tall and distinguished figure of Elizabeth Chesterton. Chesterton was an architect and town and country planner who had enrolled at the Architectural Association the year before Manasseh; her final thesis had been the design of a town for 50,000. An experimental and ambitious thinker from the outset, she took her first job in a rural planning authority and then found herself in the front line of the revolutionary comprehensive system created when the Town and Country Planning Act was passed in 1947. In a sense she was not so much the product of the new legislation as a beacon for it: able to grasp a bigger picture behind every planning problem, inventive and practical in her methodology, clear and persuasive in her recommendations, she was trusted by landowners, public bodies and designers alike.

Friends and colleagues generally remember Chesterton as 'formidable', handsome and striking in appearance; Manasseh was certainly in awe of her. It was, however, not just her personality and her ability to stay ahead in an embryonic, complex field that inspired confidence and respect. Chesterton was at ease with private rural land development on a grand scale. Although her parents' lifestyle was bohemian at times, she had been born into an established family of land surveyors and valuers.[1] She was capable of mastering all the details of a complex case, and she spoke the language of the large landowners and their newly professionalised agents. She understood their aims and their needs, and she also recognised the place of large-scale private land planning in a statutory system which had been essentially designed for public bodies and public land. She described her methods as empirical, and the key to her success with planning authorities was that she could convince them at an early stage of the negotiations that they shared a common practical goal with her clients. In so doing, she clearly foresaw the benefits of a partnership between these private owners and the mechanisms of the state. In developing private parks for public enjoyment, for example, or in reducing the problems of through-traffic in villages, such collaborations could result in the kind of benefit that the political reformers of the early 20th century had dreamed of but had been unable to execute in practice.

Chesterton was born in Hampstead Garden Suburb on 12 October 1915. Her father was the architect Maurice Chesterton, who is best known as the employer of Elizabeth Whitworth Scott with whom she went into partnership after winning the competition in 1926 for the Shakespeare Memorial Theatre at Stratford-upon-Avon. Elizabeth Chesterton's parents travelled around Wales and the Southwest in a gypsy caravan,

and she was, like Manasseh, a keen rider. Early memories from these trips not only instilled in her a respect for the countryside that was perhaps unusual in fashionable urban architects, but also gave her a sense of the relationship between the planned and the unplanned, the natural and the devised. Her first job, from 1940, was as Assistant County Planning Officer at East Suffolk. In 1947, she entered the newly created development control office of Cambridgeshire County Council as its head, studying village problems and their solutions – a pioneer role for a woman at the time. This brought her into contact with William Holford, the author of the first development plan for the city of Cambridge. Four years later, she joined him at the Social Research Unit at University College London where she worked with the German-born Marxist sociologist Ruth Glass on a study into the fairness of the new planning system. In 1954, she launched her own practice as a planning consultant – working at first for solicitors, estate agents and private clients on permissions and appeals.

In that same year, Chesterton also started to teach at the AA. Now working alongside Manasseh, she liked and respected him but they had no real contact with each other until the Civic Trust commissioned Manasseh to design a facelift for Hampstead town centre in 1961.[2] Realising that Chesterton was a Hampstead resident and the Secretary of the Old Hampstead Society, the local amenity group, he plucked up

above **Elizabeth Chesterton, photographed in the late 1980s by Hans H. Helweg.**

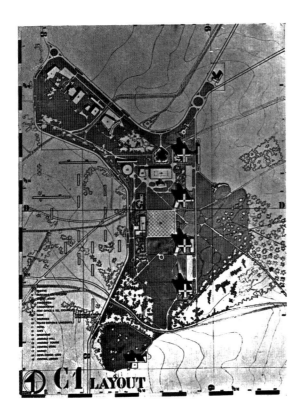

courage to approach her at the school. As it turned out, her assistance and persuasive
powers proved critical in getting the project moving – the removal of some public
lavatories frequented by taxi drivers having been especially unpopular. Soon after, when
she was working on her first large project, a look at the planning and traffic problems
of central Hereford, Manasseh offered her a partnership. Preferring to maintain her
independence, she declined; but she henceforth appeared on the architects' office
writing paper as 'consultant', and when the practice moved to Rathbone Street she took
a room of her own at the rear of the building.

Chesterton found the atmosphere of the office congenial. Furthermore, she could
easily subcontract mapping, drawing and design work for her own projects to the
partnership. In return, she talent-spotted new young architects for it. It was Chesterton
who in 1963 brought in Michael Hopkins; she had been his second-year tutor, a 'liber-
ating experience' for him.[3] As time went by, her own assistants joined her. One of the
closest and, intermittently, longest-serving of these was Susan Bell, also a friend. Bell
later made a distinguished career in rural land-use policy and practice in her own

above **Tomorrow Town: Chesterton's 4th/5th year project of 1937/38, designed with Peter Cocke and others.**

right, eventually becoming Chief Executive of the National Forest. At the same time, Chesterton shared some of her assistants with Manasseh and Ian Baker, or 'borrowed' theirs – so the office overall became an interdisciplinary one. In addition, Chesterton worked when required with external landscape architects such as Hal Moggridge (from 1969, the partner of Brenda Colvin). The result was that a client with complex planning needs could find at Leonard Manasseh & Partners all they needed at a single address. For her part Chesterton, who had trained as an architect, was sympathetic to the role of architecture in bringing about an overall planning solution. As Bell put it, Chesterton saw design as another way of 'making things work'; buildings were thus as much a component of her planning strategy as the methodologies she and Bell devised and executed together.

King's Lynn and other schemes

It was probably her experience at Hereford that led Chesterton to be recommended by Holford when the planning committee of Norfolk County Council, working with King's Lynn Borough Council, came to choose a consultant planner for the town in April 1963. The terms of reference required her to carry out a survey of the historic core of the town and to make recommendations for the preservation of existing buildings, or their modification or demolition in order 'to enhance the street scene'. This in itself is significant: by 1963, some historic towns had already planned or carried out redevelopment schemes that gave priority to vehicular traffic over historic fabric, in many cases resulting in more than local controversy. At Canterbury, an aggressive wartime demolition and rebuilding scheme had been swiftly rejected by voters, and the result had been for the most part an unhappy compromise between modernity and pastiche. In Norwich, a proposed inner link road was at the time seen by some as a symbol of the threat to the city's character as a whole. King's Lynn, which had been a prosperous centre for shipbuilding and a major port for cloth and coal before the railways diverted their trade elsewhere, had been earmarked for expansion as an overspill town for London after the Second World War, and housing estates were being planned and built around its periphery. There was, as there remains, a striking contrast between these and the dense, largely 15th- and 16th-century centre around the notable early English Palladian Customs House. Recent competitions had been held for infill buildings in this area, suggesting considerable local initiative and awareness, but an inner ring road was being planned to run along King Street and Queen Street, the length of the 'spine' comprising the historic city fabric.

Chesterton's plan, which was published in June 1964, pointed out that it was impossible to preserve the historic core while also building an 8.5 metre (28 foot)-wide ring road through the centre of it. Citing the planner Max Lock's comment that 'a town that loses its ancient buildings or a man his memory, know neither who they are nor where they belong', she called for the preservation of buildings that faced the existing streets. These included the Guildhall and the courthouse in the Saturday Market to the north

side of St Margaret's parish church, and the unusual houses in St Margaret's Place to
the west of it – some with structures and interiors that had developed over centuries.[4]
Chesterton wanted to keep existing trees, too, and her report recognised the value of
the spaces between the existing buildings, suggesting that local 'fear of the new' (as she
put it) was really a fear of the disruption of the largely intact building lines and heights.[5]
New work 'must take into account the way in which neighbouring buildings are articulated; its materials must be of a colour, texture and quality that will be complementary
to what is already there, and the refinement of detail to be found in the best existing
work must be maintained'.[6] Finally, she recognised the importance of traditional
building skills, particularly where new infill work was required.

In some respects the report was, nevertheless, a modernist one: Chesterton
envisaged a four-storey car park to replace a run-down warehousing area at the centre
of the historic town, with ramps leading up to it passing alongside the Customs House.
She also allowed the possibility of buildings up to 30.48 metres (100 feet) tall along the
waterfront. However, her overall principles – the emphasis on the continuity of historic
spaces; the value given to materials, detailing and planting; and the rejection of the
county's through-route approach to road design – were the ones that triumphed in the
end. Thus the adoption of this report by the county council could be seen as a watershed
in the protection and planning of historic towns. King's Lynn did not go the same way as
Canterbury, Worcester or many others, and its historic centre has remained intact. The
major traffic artery was in the end positioned about 400 metres (440 yards) further east,

above Ian Baker's drawing of the King's Lynn Law Courts.

and the multi-storey car park was shelved in favour of ground-level parking. Chesterton encouraged public authorities to site new public amenities in central areas of the town, rather than in the greenfield suburban sites they generally preferred in this period, and this was to some extent realised when the partnership designed the magistrates' and crown courts, completed in 1981, on the waterfront behind St Margaret's Place. The building, designed 'almost entirely' by Baker, also went some way towards showing how even a large new public building that was sensitive to local materials, forms, heights and volumes, and which was carefully and thoughtfully detailed, could contribute to the character of a historical environment without threatening it.[7] Located on South Quay, the building is broken down into a series of four volumes on a scale more typical of the Tudor fabric of the quayside than of the structures they replaced. The composition is, however, drawn into a coherent whole by the narrow tower, the homogeneity of the materials and their careful junctions – especially around the bases of the windows (detailed by Alex Billeter) along College Lane to the north.

Infill work of this kind was rare for the practice. In a competition held in 1975 to design a bar and party rooms on the site of a bathhouse and workshops at the southern tip of Magdalen College, Oxford, they were shortlisted but lost to Maguire & Murray. The partners' scheme, surprisingly, included new Gothic windows and battlements. A 1976 scheme by Chesterton for the town centre of Chippenham in Wiltshire aimed, like that for King's Lynn, at solving traffic problems without damaging the historic fabric of the town and at identifying opportunities for both conservation and growth.

above **King's Lynn Law Courts, photographed by Martin Charles in 1981.**

Although implemented, the scheme did not provide any architectural commissions. A similar small-scale conservation project for the Old Market area of Bristol, for the city council and Bristol Municipal Charities, did on the other hand result in the design of some residential buildings at Redcross Street. The motivation for these urban plans was usually the need of a town authority to find a statutory basis for attracting grants for restoring historical buildings.[8]

Analogous with the King's Lynn proposals, another scheme for a highly sensitive site again saw an overall concept prepared by Chesterton with the partnership providing a building to suit it. This time it was for the summit of Mount Snowdon, then occupied by the already unsatisfactory concrete building of 'devastating banality' (according to Chesterton) that had been designed by Clough Williams-Ellis in 1934.[9] Chesterton's scheme, for the Countryside Commission and published in 1975, considered the future of the area and its tourist-development potential as a whole. It was radical for the time in that it envisaged a site that could be used all year round by harnessing and at the same time recording solar energy. The current tourist use of the summit was monitored by Bell, who was sent up there to carry out a survey, and it was for this project that Chesterton, aware that a landscape architect was needed, worked with Moggridge for the first time. The partnership provided the design for a new building to replace Williams-Ellis's – a scheme thought by several of the architects in the office to be one of the best of all its unexecuted ones – and a dramatic aerial perspective by Baker, hung in the reception lobby, greeted visitors to the Rathbone Street offices for some time after any possibility of its being implemented had faded.

above Ian Baker's aerial perspective of the Snowdon scheme.

The 1947 Planning Act, and much legislation that developed in its aftermath (such as the Countryside Act of 1968, enabling the creation of country parks by local authorities), encouraged large-scale planning by public bodies. Although Chesterton was in many ways representative of both this era and its values, some of her most remarkable work was in fact carried out for private landowners. Two projects for Foster Yeoman, a large quarrying firm founded in the West Country in 1949, illustrate how Chesterton and Manasseh addressed the problems that companies faced when planning substantial new industrial facilities that were potentially harmful to the environment. They needed now to supply local authorities with professionally prepared master plans that showed how they intended to ameliorate the impact of their work. The first of the Foster Yeoman plans was carried out at Torr Quarry in 1977, at a sensitive site in the East Mendips in Somerset where the draft county planning policy at the time recommended a long-term master plan for its development. The quarry was within an area defined as having 'great landscape value', and furthermore the factory area itself was alongside a Site of Special Scientific Interest and other areas of protected woodland. The scheme was thus necessarily one which required a broad spectrum of professional skills, and the partnership's report covered every aspect of the quarry's operations and layout. Baker designed a lightweight glazed structure that sat elegantly over the railway tracks. His close friend, the graphic designer James Sutton, provided bold lettering and signage for the main entrance from the road, and a series of standard details was prepared by Moggridge for use across the site. 'Let others follows suit', said the

above left **James Sutton's sign at the entrance to Torr Quarry, Somerset. The scheme set a new standard for industrial uses in sensitive sites.**
above right **The railhead building.**

Architects' Journal: 'This sort of initiative and care should be widely copied and, indeed, made mandatory by every planning authority on every quarry-owner.'

Foster Yeoman was a pioneer of the use of rail transport for aggregates; these travelled along tracks from the quarries to railheads where the loads were transferred onto lorries. Following the Torr project, Chesterton and the partnership designed one of these rail/road transfer schemes at Theale, in Berkshire west of Reading. The

above top Theale Depot, Berkshire: one end of the 230-metre (755-foot) building.
above A view showing the long hipped roofs.

structure housing the operations – a very long, tall building, mainly roof and with a curved ridge – seems more like an agricultural shed than an industrial plant. A wedge of planting isolates it from neighbouring housing. At the time, there was considerable interest in developing what were termed 'megaquarries' or 'superquarries' – that is, the concentration of regional quarrying works into a single well-planned site in order to minimise impact. The partnership carried out a further environmental study and plan for an operation like this, for Yeoman (Morvern) Ltd, at Glensanda on Loch Linnhe on the west coast of Scotland. The idea was that the quarry would be served only by sea with no road links at all, and that all the operations would be largely within the hill itself and therefore hidden from view when looking out north-west from the mainland coast around Oban. It is engaging to discover that present-day tourists are astonished to come across this hidden place; its site was very carefully chosen. The reputation of the partnership in this field was such that by the 1980s it received a number of commissions for large, unexciting, but well-paying infrastructure projects in problematic sites.

Beaulieu

None of these schemes had, however, anything like the significance or impact of the partnership's work for Lord Montagu of Beaulieu from 1966. The Beaulieu scheme as eventually executed included master planning on a grand scale as well as detailed layouts; buildings of different sizes, including both a huge pavilion and various smaller interventions of remarkable subtlety; and landscaping and planting designs, which have now reached maturity. The result is a formal, visionary scheme quite the equal of any carried out by a dynastic landowner anywhere in Europe, at any time since the days of the great formal landscape gardens of the 18th century.

Chesterton was able to cultivate traditional landowners with her considerable flair for communicating modern planning problems and solutions in a language that seemed both authoritative and reasonable. In fact, the skill very often lay not so much in dealing with the landowners themselves as with their agents and managers. The need to maintain a large inherited agricultural estate – perhaps not a very well run one – during an era which was by and large unfavourable to inherited wealth and old-fashioned practices had forced a new degree of professionalism on landowners, and so they in turn appointed agents with the experience and training now required to look after their estates. At Harewood near Leeds, prolonged contact between the estate and the partnership failed to result in any significant work, perhaps because the agent was never able to carry out the leadership role required to get a large project off the ground. At Beaulieu, on the other hand, the project benefited from the role played by Montagu's agent. Seconded from the surveyors and valuers Strutt & Parker, Brian Hubbard saw that the various elements of so ambitious a project formed part of a coordinated scheme.

The critical figure, however, was Edward Douglas-Scott-Montagu, third Baron Montagu of Beaulieu, who never failed to provide the enthusiasm and the backing that the scheme required. Kenneth Robinson, the Managing Director of Montagu Ventures Ltd. who joined the project in 1969 just before the final decision to proceed was taken, has no doubt that Montagu was the pathfinder, at times adamant that it should go ahead even when consultants had advised otherwise.

Lord Montagu's father, the second Baron, had died when he was a small child and he had entered into his responsibilities in the running of his estate immediately on his coming of age with a youthful enthusiasm and imagination that was rare in the post-war economic climate. His family had possessed the Beaulieu Estate around the Beaulieu River, a tributary of the Solent to the south-west of Southampton, since it had been sold off at the Reformation in 1538. Towards the northern end of the estate lay former Cistercian abbey buildings. Close to these was Palace House, the residence designed by Sir Arthur Blomfield for the first Baron Montagu in 1871. The second Baron Montagu, born in 1866, had been fascinated by mechanical engineering. First of all steam locomotives had interested him; then, in the 1890s, he took up motoring, participating in early car races and promoting the use of cars to the royal family and politicians.

The third Baron Montagu was, like his father, a motoring enthusiast. Although it may have been financial motives that required him to open his house to the public in April 1952, he soon realised that it was possible to establish the place as a tourist destination by sharing his love of cars with his visitors. First he exhibited his collection of vehicles within the house itself, but by 1956 they had been transferred into 'two large sheds in the garden'. The number of cars began to expand, and a more substantial purpose-built construction was opened to exhibit them in 1959. Montagu had a natural flair for showmanship, hosting rallies, races and festivals at Beaulieu. These were always well publicised, and sometimes attended by well-known personalities, and by 1961 his museum and house had received 1.4 million visitors. Two years later, there was a summer peak of 8,000 a day.[10] Beaulieu was second only to the Tower of London in terms of its visitor numbers. As Bill Swallow later put it for *Building Design*, even before the new museum was opened Beaulieu was outperforming its rival stately homes, Woburn and Longleat, 'in every way without even resorting to lions and the smell of frying onions'.

This in itself was a problem for the estate: access to Palace House, Beaulieu Abbey and the existing museum was possible only from the south, and most traffic had to negotiate a difficult corner at the head of Beaulieu village or pass through the narrow and congested village street to get there. Within the grounds visitors had to drive through the middle of the historic sites, mixing awkwardly with pedestrians, and facilities such as refreshments were badly squeezed. Queues were forming all over the place: to get in, to park, to see the collection, to eat, even to get out (although not for the lavatories, which were unusually generous). Any expansion of the museum – and the collection itself was still growing – would further threaten the attractive setting which made a visit there part of a pleasant day out. It was this basic problem that required a plan. Yet the atmosphere of 1960s planning did not favour an isolated solution. In order to approve expansion of the museum, the local and county authorities would require an

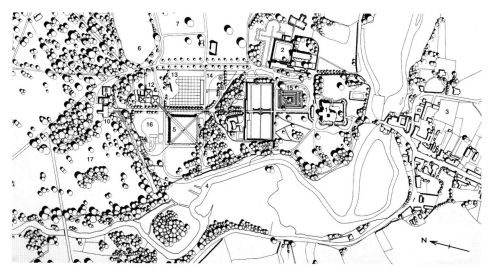

Key
1   Palace House
2   The Abbey
3   Beaulieu village
4   Beaulieu river
5   The Motor Museum

6   Vineyard
7   Car rally area
8   Library
9   Offices
10 Information centre
11 Lecture hall

12 Restaurants
13 Test track
14 Open air exhibition
15 The maze
16 Summertime diversions
17 Car parking

investigation into traffic routes and detailed parking proposals; they would want to see a forecast of the economic impact of the increased tourism on the employment situation of the area; and they would have expected a developer to indicate what the impact would be on places that were economically linked to the project site. As it was, other aspects of the Beaulieu Estate also needed review, including the shipbuilding village of Buckler's Hard with its pair of 18th-century terraces, maritime museum and hotel; the boating facilities on the Beaulieu River; and longer-term housing plans. In this era of comprehensive and centralised regional planning – with Hampshire's own county development plan revised in 1961, and a new study by Colin Buchanan into the traffic problems of the area already under way – any ambitious development would necessitate an overall plan.

Hubbard, Montagu's agent, must have recognised that modern planning required not only vision and competency but also a complete familiarity with these complex modern statutory planning processes. He had learned to appreciate Chesterton's skills when she had designed a scheme for the centre of Dartington, near Totnes, which in the end had not been executed. Chesterton later remarked that the first time Strutt & Parker had approached her to act for them, in connection with another site, she had turned them down because she did not agree with the principle of the consent they wanted; if anything this had increased their respect for her.[11] Thus it came about

above **Beaulieu, Hampshire: the master plan.**

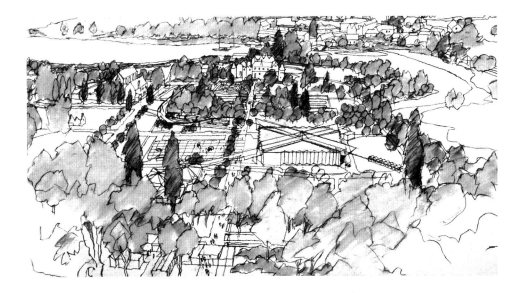

that 'Elizabeth Chesterton in association with Leonard Manasseh and Partners' was commissioned in the spring of 1965 to produce the 20-year Beaulieu Development Plan, later (and significantly) named the Beaulieu Conservation Plan. From this were to flow the architectural and landscape interventions that were to make up the partnership's masterpiece. The plan eventually formed part of Hampshire's county development plan, the first time a privately conceived initiative was adopted in this way.

Montagu knew very little about the architects who were part of the 'package' when he first appointed Chesterton, but it is likely that he was reassured about their abilities by Basil Spence who in 1958 had built himself a house by the Beaulieu River. Another neighbour who probably put in more than a word for them was Hugh Casson, Manasseh's supporter since the Festival of Britain, who had a cottage on the estate and knew Montagu well. As both Manasseh and Chesterton later recalled, Montagu proved to be a remarkable client. Although he maintained an iron grip on the budget, for example refusing to countenance any contingency costs, he gave the architects complete freedom to design as they pleased. The only occasion on which he expressed any anxiety about their concept was in their choice of orange for the painted steelwork in the museum building, and even on this the architects managed to get their own way.

The scheme proposed covered about 44 hectares (110 acres) of the site and established a grand axis – *'Beaux Arts'* was how the architects described it – that ran about 500 metres (550 yards) in a straight line south (actually, south-south-east) towards Palace House. Visitors would park at the far northern end and make their way on foot through the site, passing all the new facilities and commercial activities at the near end before

above Ian Baker's aerial perspective of the Beaulieu master plan, looking south from the museum (centre-right) to Palace House.

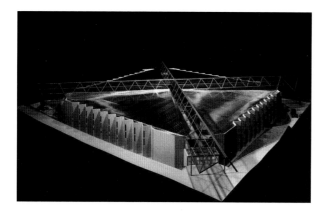

reaching the historic areas and the residence towards the south. This latter area was thus kept free of traffic. The route could only reach Palace House by piercing the northern end of an old walled garden, and a structure called 'the hole in the wall' was designed to frame the transition into this space. The axis then continued south in alignment with the historical layout of the walled garden, terminating at the clock tower of what had been a garage and shop building of 1960. A monorail was to snake around these areas – Montagu had been impressed by the 'mini-rail' at the 1967 Montreal Expo, and had sent Manasseh and Hubbard to look at it. Various types of open ground for activities were to be located between the buildings: a 5,000-square metre (one-and-a-quarter-acre) arena alongside the museum for vehicle rallies and demonstrations; a 40,000-square metre (10-acre) area for outside events; and a further 3,000-square metre (three-quarter-acre) 'area for summertime diversions', which was to provide a location for transport-themed amusements between the entrance pavilion, the restaurant and the monorail station. There was thus a mixture of different building types right from the start – indeed, the way in which the whole complex was commissioned and designed together is itself a kind of microcosm of the contemporary practice of comprehensive planning. It is worth observing that 40 years later every one of the structures and areas continues to perform precisely the purpose originally intended for it.

The National Motor Museum was the major structure on the site. It was designed principally by Baker (who was given the lead credit by the partnership), with Christopher Hulls as project architect. John Birkett-Smith, in time an inheritor of the successor practice, cut his teeth here as a project assistant: he came directly from the end of his fifth year at the AA after his work was spotted by Chesterton at the annual exhibition of diploma projects in 1970, and it is his initials that appear on most of the surviving drawings. The building was essentially a single tall large space, maximising the flexibility of the display area, and with the plan of a square with serrated edges. The sides of the square are 63.40 metres (208 feet) long, so the building covers over 4,000

above **The partnership's model of the National Motor Museum.**

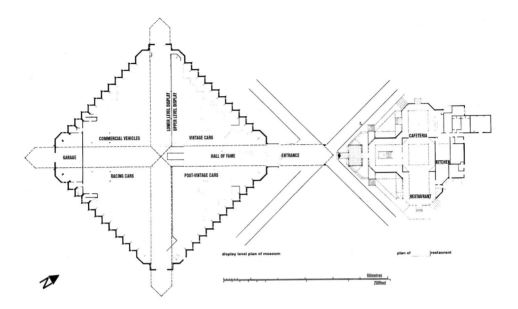

square metres (almost an acre). Some parts of the interior have two levels, and thus
the building as a whole can accommodate nearly 6,500 square metres (70,000 square
feet) of display space. It is therefore clear that one of the challenges of its design was to
ensure that its considerable bulk could sit comfortably within what was always intended
to be both an attractive, verdant landscape and also a kind of large-scale formal garden.

Baker and his team, including the structural engineers Felix J. Samuely & Partners,
broke down any potential bulkiness using three devices. The most significant of these
was the exploitation of levels so that visitors approached a building that seemed lower
than it was; in addition, the building was first seen from one of its corners. Secondly,
there was to be a tall glazed roof, which sat above the flat roof that covered most of the
hall and stretched like an extended 'X' between and beyond the corners of the square.
The final form of this element emerged once the monorail idea had been adopted.
Thirdly, the building's size would be visually broken down internally through the
manipulation of the plan of the external walls, and the use of colour and columns.
The overall strategy was to provide a space that actually had about it something of the
fun (for the spectator, at any rate) of a busy garage. It says something about his own
approach to his project that Montagu populated the model for it, made by Manasseh's
son Zac, with Matchbox toy cars from the museum's collection.

Visitors enter through a grand portico formed by the extension of the glazed
roof beyond the north-east corner of the building into a darkened 'Hall of Fame'.
They find themselves on an upper level, from which they can look out over the tall
space of the whole of the museum. From here they descend half a storey into the

above The ground-floor plan of the National Motor Museum (left) and Brabazon Restaurant (right).

double-height part of the hall, facing the motorcycle gallery opposite. The glazed roof soars above the whole of the square hall, its open painted steel trusses sitting on slender, widely spaced columns. Its 'busyness' does not detract from the space below, in part because of the strong geometry of its overall forms but also because its components belong so unmistakably to the visual language of motor garages: the orange paintwork the architects had insisted on seems to have been the right choice. The brilliance of the internal display layout was that the cars were presented at 45 degrees to the visitor, giving a much more interesting view of, and beyond, each vehicle. The monorail runs along one of the two diagonal axes, and so there is a further row of dark green columns supporting its track across the centre. The external walls, stiffened by the serrated plan, are built from dense aggregate Forticrete fairfaced concrete blocks, of a yellow-grey colour. Within the building they disappear entirely, as do the brown brindle paviors underfoot. Finally, these angled walls with their arrow-slit windows allow daylight to illuminate the cars only indirectly, thus preserving their paintwork from the sun. The overall effect of walking into the centre of the building with its carefully lit exhibits is thus not unlike stepping into the treasury of a medieval castle. Casson advised on the internal displays – a difficult job because several different car-component makers provided their own exhibits – mainly along the length of the storage-area wall that faced directly into the lower part of the hall. The Hall of Fame itself was sponsored by

above **The National Motor Museum: interior view looking north from the cycle gallery.**

above top The castle-like Forticrete walls of the National Motor Museum.
above Looking along the west wall of the museum from the monorail entrypoint at the south-west corner.

Alcan, the aluminium manufacturers; Montagu had persuaded them to transfer their promotional strategy from golf to motor cars.

On the other side of the main north–south route, opposite the entrance portico to the museum and sharing its diagonal axis, is the Brabazon Restaurant building, for which Manasseh was himself the principal designer. This is planned in the form of a Greek cross, of which the rear bar forms the kitchen. The main eating space is thus T-shaped with chamfered corners and glazed along most of its sides, maximising the variety of views from it across to the museum or towards the entrance, the monorail station and the continuation of the main vista towards Palace House. The result is that the building feels as if it is located within a park, even though it is actually adjacent to a large exhibition hall. You can enter the Brabazon from any of the glazed walls, but the main entrance is up a flight of stairs leading from the side that faces the museum portico. In fact these two porticos seem almost to nod to one another, creating a gentle rippling effect across the axis. The restaurant roof stacks up from the outside towards the centre of the cross of the plan in low glazed stages.

The other Beaulieu structures are very much smaller, but no less sophisticated. Manasseh told Robinson, Montagu's manager, that the idea was one of 'glass buildings

above **The adjacent porch canopies of the Brabazon Restaurant (left) and National Motor Museum (right).**

in parkland, in the tradition of Decimus Burton'. The old walled garden of Beaulieu houses a large lean-to greenhouse related to this family of buildings. The new structures stand along the grand route that runs through the scheme, sharing with each other and the museum a number of common features including portico-like glazed gables and roofs, and brightly coloured steelwork. They include the entrance and exit pavilion, with a shop attached, and the adjacent John Montagu Building containing administrative offices and the Motor Museum Libraries. The smallest intervention along the route is Manasseh's 'hole in the wall' at the crossing point into the old walled garden – another open, glazed portico that rises above decorative walls built from engineering brick.

The landscape planning holds the scheme together as much as the buildings do. The landscape architect for the planting and detailed design was J. St Bodfan Gruffydd, with Derek Lovejoy & Partners retained for the garden areas around Palace House itself. In order that most traffic could enter the site without going through the village of Beaulieu, Chesterton created a new bypass. Entry to the site was now provided via a four-lane bridge over the Beaulieu River away from the village and to the west of the new north entry pavilion. Parking for 1,500 cars was distributed around small irregular car parks, often with old trees left untouched; the partnership referred to this as 'sculpting' the existing woods to accommodate them. From north to south, buildings and open spaces were separated from the central axial route by plain grassed banks formed with soil excavated for the major structures. These separate the concessions

above The Brabazon Restaurant from the porch of the National Motor Museum.

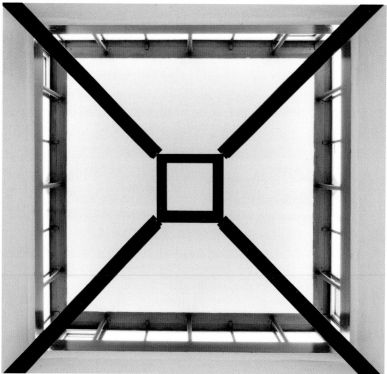

above top **The interior of the Brabazon Restaurant.**
above **Looking up towards the pyramid roof in the Brabazon Restaurant.**

above top The entry pavilion, from the north.
above Interior of the boardroom, John Montagu Building.

above top The northern monorail station.
above The monorail enters the National Motor Museum.

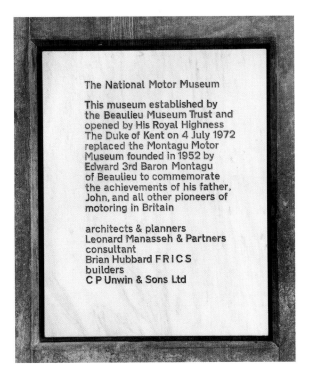

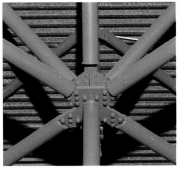

and summer attractions area from the museum and main route, and have the quality of the remains of defensive ramparts around a fortress. Graphic design across the project was, as at Torr, by James Sutton, and display fittings inside were designed by the partnership and Dennis Brennan. As Ralph Montagu, Lord Montagu's son, points out, this type of visual coordination was in marked contrast to that at most visitor attractions of the day.

Construction of the museum began in December 1970, and the complex was opened by the Duke of Kent in July 1972. The professional press in Britain and abroad covered the buildings in detail. It was reported with a great deal of photography soon after opening not only in the *Architectural Review, Building, Building Design, Architectural Design* and *Design* (the magazine of the Design Council), but also in *Architecture d'Aujourd'hui, Bauen und Wohnen, Domus* and the Danish *Arkitekten*. Specialist publications also covered it: *Tubular Structures, Brick Bulletin, Building with Steel* and, eventually, *Landscape Design*. It was thus the project which received wider coverage than any other by the partnership. It won an RIBA Southern Region award in 1973, and in 1974 both the National Heritage 'Museum of the Year' award and a steel award from the British Steel Corporation and the British Constructional Steelwork Association. It

above top left **The marble plaque commemorating the opening of the National Motor Museum in 1972.**
above top right **The National Motor Museum: steelwork details.**

also won a third prize in the Royal Institution of Chartered Surveyors (RICS) and *The Times* Conservation Awards.

There was a rumour in the partnership's office that Manasseh himself had had to exert his charm in order to get the editor of the *Architectural Review* to publish a more flattering description of the project than that originally offered by his correspondent. The published article by Lance Wright offered the insight that Beaulieu's success was due to the fact that it was as much 'fairground' as museum, and that consequently it benefited from its busyness and its 'constant glimpses of alternate joys'. Wright regretted, however, the future dustiness of all those rolled steeled joists (a component 'created by the visually blind'). This emphasis on the fairground aspect of the scheme was perhaps due to the sober nature of other recent car museums. Swallow's piece in *Building Design* referred by way of contrast to the recent Daimler Benz museum in Stuttgart, where any sense of the working garage had evidently been banished in favour of a sophisticatedly technological architectural language. Similarly, the number of *Design* that reviewed Beaulieu also carried an article about a car museum designed by Studios DA and PRF and completed in 1971 for Gianni Mazzocchi, the editor of *Domus*, as part of the magazine's office complex on the outskirts of Milan. This building, too, was constructed in steel and glass, and with aluminium patent glazing, but it exemplified a particularly austere kind of modern good taste. The vehicles were arranged in an unrelenting grid inside.

above **The Master Builder's House Hotel in Buckler's Hard, soon after completion.**

Wright acknowledged the way in which the patent-glazed roofs throughout the scheme linked the Beaulieu buildings together as a family, tracing their origins to the lean-to roofs that shelter the weekend washers of cars. The author of the piece in *Architecture d'Aujourd'hui* recognised the intended references to the types of structures that are associated with grand 19th-century gardens such as Burton's Palm House, or even the Crystal Palace. Perhaps the fact that the National Motor Museum was so successful as a 'fairground', to use Wright's expression, obscured its success in making a coherent, formal architecture out of the contemporary technological elements of car architecture, creating a symbolic language that at the same time refers back to the great dynastic gardens of earlier generations. The pair of 'nodding' glazed gables that bridge the museum and the restaurant building and the echoes of them in structures like the hole in the wall ('built to amuse', according to the architects) are at least as effective in evoking a landscape of woods and temples as any Neoclassical scheme. Down in Buckler's Hard, on the river to the south-east of the museum complex, the partnership extended the small Master Builder's Hotel with an elegant 18-room block in stripy red and pink brick which was admired by a local resident because it looked as if it had always been there. Manasseh told a journalist in 1973 that 'there could be no higher praise as far as we were concerned'.[12] However, even that little block originally had a tiny glass canopy and portico, with a steelwork frame, making it as much part of the overall concept of the master plan as if it had been a thematic grotto in the corner of a garden by Kent or Bridgeman.

Other planning-led projects

Montagu was satisfied with the new complex and remained on friendly terms with the architects. To the regret of both, however, constructional problems with the glazing and roofing over the museum, which led to an out-of-court settlement, resulted in the architects' insurers preventing them from working for the same client again. For that reason, the two substantial later buildings on the site near the entrance pavilion were designed by other architects. While the project was going on, however, its designers found themselves extremely busy. Just after Beaulieu was opened, Chesterton said she had around 20 planning projects in the pipeline. Her roles on public bodies and committees, such as the National Trust and the RFAC, also brought work her way. Sometimes these were for purely rural planning, such as her proposal of 1967, with Michael Dower, to establish a country park over 280 hectares (692 acres) alongside the 'Seven Sisters', the famous chalk cliffs of East Sussex.[13] Cases like these were occasionally controversial locally, because the public (and their local newspapers) were yet to discover that the term 'country park' did not necessarily entail rowdy tourist development. The Beaulieu plan had proved contentious locally, and, even with the support of planners, it had taken a public enquiry to get permission for it.

In some cases, Chesterton's long-term planning projects resulted in architectural commissions for Manasseh and Baker. In 1966 the partnership prepared another study

and plan for Dartington, and the following year designed on Dartington Hall Trust land the first phase of a residential estate. Set around a square of open grassland close to the early 20th-century house of Hunters Moon, the houses were located at the southern end of the village itself. The white rendered buildings have the tall monopitch gables and geometrical, loosely gridded window patterns that are characteristic of the office's work. At the northern end of the village and on the edge of a public car park close to the entrance drive to the Hall, Manasseh designed a circular public lavatory, now demolished, a building he was particularly proud of – perhaps always mindful of the way in which his career had been launched by a block of public conveniences on the South Bank.[14] He thus joined a select group of distinguished architects who had made tiny interventions near this site, from A. W. N. Pugin (who added a single chimney to the Hall in 1846), to Walter Gropius and William Lescaze.

In terms of providing work for the office as a whole, the most significant employer of all the private landowners was probably the Trustees of the Chatsworth Settlement, the present-day incorporation of the landholdings of the Duke of Devonshire.[15] The Settlement owned considerable tranches of property in and around Eastbourne in East Sussex, and these were developed in different ways. Chesterton was involved with some minor schemes, such as that at Birling Gap, a tourist outlook point close by Beachy Head affected by coastal erosion; the partnership also designed new units for

above A house at Hunters Moon at Dartington, Devon, photographed in 2010.

an industrial estate near Eastbourne. The most interesting of these schemes was for a marina development at the Crumbles, 160 hectares (395 acres) of worked-out coastal shingle just east of the town centre. A total of 2,500 units were designed on irregularly shaped quays and islands. Birkett-Smith designed house types and made an elaborate model, but in retrospect the scheme was, he said, too 'Rolls Royce' for the local market, and the project was built in a much simplified form.[16]

Wellington Country Park

The partnership did, however, undertake one further large-scale planning and design project that was executed in its entirety: the pioneering Wellington Country Park in Berkshire, near the home of the Dukes of Wellington at Stratfield Saye. Hubbard was again a consultant for the scheme, this time acting on behalf of the eighth Duke and in partnership with his agent Christopher Scott. The Duke retired from the army in 1968, the year in which the Countryside Commission had been established to set up and promote country parks. He later wrote that he felt it was time that the 4,600-hectare (11,370-acre) estate, originally bought with a grant from parliament to the first Duke in 1817 in recognition of his defeat of Napoleon, 'should come to terms with what was happening in the outside world'. Baker recalled that the partnership thought that Wellington was aware of the developing project at Beaulieu, and wanted to show that he too could create an impressive scheme. In fact, the situation at Stratfield Saye was quite unlike that at Beaulieu: there was no established attraction, and no need for a

above **The proposed marina at the Crumbles, Eastbourne, East Sussex.**

large-scale built facility. The area designated for the plan, 243 hectares (600 acres), was important as a green 'lung' in an area that was being rapidly built over. It lay near Riseley, not far south from the junction between the M3 motorway and the A32 which links Reading with Basingstoke, and it was more likely to function as a day out for town and city dwellers than as an exciting holiday attraction. Planted with oak, beech, birch and pine, the only distinctive existing landscape feature was a former gravel pit at the north-east corner. The intention here, then, was to convert an unremarkable piece of land into a place which would have sufficient rural interest to attract the population round about. It was also recognised at the time that the appeal of the park would be enhanced by the fact that Stratfield Saye house itself, a short distance away by car, would be opened to the public. Thus this plan required inventing new things to do within the landscape, such as boating, picnicking, coarse fishing, canoeing, and the provision of children's play sites. The gravel pit was converted into a lake, extensive car parks were 'sculpted' into the woodlands as they had been at Beaulieu, and paths led visitors to the various activities. A caravan park was established in the south-east of the site, again 'sculpted' between the trees (the caravans themselves are today scarcely visible in aerial photographs).

The partnership designed the three buildings that completed the scheme: an information centre, a restaurant by the edge of the lake and a central facilities structure for the caravan site housing showers, lavatories and a launderette. The project architect

above **The visitors' information centre at Wellington Country Park, Berkshire.**

throughout was John Thake, and the graphics were again by Sutton. The idea here
was to design the structures using a consistent grid, with steel box sections for
columns and a kit of glued laminated timber members for the roofs so that all these
elements could be extended or changed as circumstances developed. The estate's
own workforce built the project, the Duke himself taking a strong personal interest.
At the time, flexibility in tourist planning was considered essential – the more so
in a situation where demand was being created from scratch. The information block
and restaurant were designed on a six-metre (19 foot 8 inch) grid, with large slate
pyramidal roofs over clusters of four squares for major public spaces, and smaller
ones over other areas. Junctions between the members of the roof were achieved with
simple steel brackets, which for Lance Wright, visiting for the *Architectural Review*
in 1975, this time achieved a 'pleasant, monumental effect'. As he pointed out, the
structures were competing for attention with the landscape which had been created
around them. The substantial nature of the few basic materials used in their design
gave them a permanence which, for all the windows that filled their walls, made them
more than transitory park pavilions. Looking out from within was, he said, as if you
'were peering out from under a large umbrella'.

The structures have survived in their original form, just like those at Beaulieu
– the restaurant pavilion was to have been extended but has remained its original
size. The conviction by landscape and tourism planners that flexibility was of vital

above **The restaurant by the lake.**

importance seems in retrospect to have been itself part of the atmosphere of the times. For the design of the park, the partnership won the European Architectural Heritage Year Award in 1975, and this time managed second prize in the RICS and *The Times* Conservation Awards of the same year. It seems very probable that the scheme was seen as a model for future public parks: in 1978, when summarising the first ten years of the Countryside Act, the Countryside Commission's landscape architect Paul Walshe drew particular attention to Wellington and Beaulieu. He pointed to the characteristics which had made these two schemes so successful: the way in which their design had been part of a broad regional planning strategy; the existence of detailed management plans, which in the nature of things were more typical of the private sector than of public parks; and the fact that this new type of leisure development was intended itself to have an educational aspect to it. Visitors would learn to appreciate the countryside more, and likewise the park's strategy would be to bring about a more 'caring community'. The Wellington Country Park did this not only through educational displays, but also through the wide range of activities it offered. So in a sense the park buildings, large and small, continued where the '51 Bar (in common with other buildings of the Festival of Britain) had started: small, elegant, leisurely structures,

above **The staff compound on Hampstead Heath, London, designed by Phineas Manasseh, 1990–2.**

conceived as parts of a much larger whole, each making discreet statements about modern life, its duties and its pleasures. These themes were central to the partnership's approach to architecture throughout the whole of its existence. It was perhaps more than paternal pride which led Manasseh to say of one of his very last projects, the small staff compound on the east side of Hampstead Heath completed for the Corporation of the City of London in 1992 and for which his son Phin was project architect, that this was 'one of our better little buildings'.[17]

Notes

1   Chesterton described her family and early life in her interviews with Louise Brodie, 1997, 'Architects' Lives', British Library Sound Archive, reference C467/25 [Chesterton BL interviews], Tape 1 Side A. Susan Bell (11 October 2009) and John Birkett-Smith have also provided much valuable information; see also the biographical file at the RIBA Library.

2   Referred to in Manasseh BL interviews, Tape 4 Side B; author's interview with David Etherton, 5 February 2010.

3   Author's conversation with Sir Michael Hopkins, 10 November 2009; his email message, 12 March 2010.

4   E. U. Chesterton in association with Leonard Manasseh & Partners, *The Historic Core of King's Lynn, a Study and Plan*, Norwich, Norfolk County Council, 1964, p9; quotation from Max Lock in *Architects' Journal*, 18 November 1964, p 1160. Nina Baker remembers walking with her father through the old buildings in the centre of the town, and he made sketches of some of them.

5   Chesterton in association with Leonard Manasseh & Partners, op. cit., p9.

6   ibid., p8.

7   The reference to Baker's role in the design of the building is from Manasseh BL interviews, Tape 6 Side A, supported by interviews with John Birkett-Smith and Alex Billeter.

8   This was Chesterton's judgement: Chesterton BL interviews, Tape 5 Side A.

9   Chesterton BL interviews, Tape 4 Side A.

10   In addition to the detailed descriptions in the professional publications listed in the List of Works below, further information on the Montagu family and the early museum has been derived from *Beaulieu: Beaulieu Abbey, Palace House, National Motor Museum*, Beaulieu, Beaulieu Enterprises, Ltd, written by Lord Montagu, originally published c.1983, and regularly updated. The author would like to thank Ken Robinson and Ralph Montagu for many helpful corrections to, and comments on, this section.

11   Chesterton BL interviews, Tape 4 Side A.

12   Paul Davies, 'Profile of a practice', *Architect*, August 1973, p50.

13   For the Seven Sisters report, see the case study by Andrew Thorburn, 'Planning for Leisure in the Countryside', available at http://www.jplc.org/papers/1982%20Thorburn.pdf

14   Nigel Honer recalls that the partnership also added WCs at Mitford Castle outside Bath, and may have designed other visitor arrangements there.

15   The Duke interviewed Manasseh at Beaulieu, suggesting that the connection came through Montagu. Manasseh's BL interviews Tape 2 Side A.

16   Christine Smyth and Simon Jennings, in 'Coastline Changes and Land Management in East Sussex, Southern England', *Ocean and Shoreline Management*, vol 11, Issues 4–5, 1988, pp375–94, described the project as then being currently planned. According to Manasseh BL interviews, Tape 7 Side B, Baker designed a marina for a site in the British Virgin Islands.

17   Manasseh BL interviews, Tape 2 Side A.

5   Cornice

Both Leonard Manasseh and Elizabeth Chesterton enjoyed being active members of committees and were good at it, and through the 1970s and 1980s they took on an increasing number of public roles. Chesterton, in the words of her obituarist Peter Inskip, had an ability to sound 'profound, but never daunting' on the many committees on which she served.[1] Her public career is worth recounting in some detail in order to convey its comprehensive nature: she became a Royal Fine Art Commissioner from 1970 to 1984, and thereafter a member of the first board of English Heritage (EH), chaired by Lord Montagu of Beaulieu; already a member of the Historic Buildings Council from 1973, she joined EH's Historic Buildings Advisory Committee and later its Historic Areas Advisory Committee (from 1985), remaining on the successor committees for another 12 years. She joined the National Trust's Architectural Panel in 1978; and between 1985 and 1990 was a member of its Council, nominated by the RIBA. She also served on British Rail's Environmental Panel from 1983. It was for this wide scope of activities that she was rewarded with an OBE in 1977 and was appointed Dame ten years later. Not surprisingly, the partnership benefited from her growing connections. From 1982 until 1986 the partnership carried out work for the National Trust at the recently acquired Kingston Lacy Estate in Dorset, in association with the architects Caröe and Partners. Under Chesterton's direction, John Birkett-Smith redesigned the public entry route to the house with discreet parking and a tidy access route that led visitors in through the stables, freeing the house's north-east-facing front elevation. Martin Caröe worked on the restoration of the house, and the Trust itself revived the gardens. Chesterton remained active well into her 80s, living in her parents' old house in Hampstead until her death on 18 August 2002.

Manasseh's public commitments tended to be more artistic ones. On retiring from the AA Presidency in 1965, he became a member of the Council of Industrial Design. He was elected a Fellow of the Royal Society of Arts in 1967, and was on the RIBA Council from 1968 to 1970. To this he made a remarkable comeback in 1979 when he stood with his friend John Partridge under the banner (and four-word manifesto) of the 'Hurrah for Architecture Group'. His election address, which contrasted with the generally gloomy tone of one of the RIBA's recurrent phases of introspection, claimed that 'living architecture was vital to the wellbeing of this country – of any civilised country', and that 'the British deserve better'. In the election he received 1,246 votes, top of the poll with almost as much support as the next three candidates combined, and became Honorary Secretary during his term of office.[2] He too was on the Council of the

opposite The entrance court at Forde House, Newton Abbott, Devon: the architectural treatment was by Leonard Manasseh.

above top Elizabeth Chesterton directing operations on site at Kingston Lacy, Dorset, in 1983.
above *Plage de l'Abbaye*, St. Jacut-de-la-Mer, 1962, by Leonard Manasseh.

National Trust, nominated by the Royal Academy, from 1977 until 1990, as well as the Ancient Monuments Board for England from 1978 to 1984 and the Chatham Historic Dockyard Trust from 1977.

One of the activities for which he retained the greatest affection was his role as the first architect President of the Royal West of England Academy, to which he was elected for a six-year term in 1989, and where he is remembered as a diplomatic, gentlemanly figure. A remarkable aspect of these activities was that he always remained committed to organisations well after his retirement from office might have freed him from them: in his 90s he still attended annual receptions and dinners, sometimes travelling long distances to get there. His own painting ('I am quite a good architect – I would like to be a good painter as well') and his support for contemporary artists provided another dimension to his career. He occasionally wrote about his interests in the professional press, including a description of the Society of Architect-Artists (architects 'should all join at once').[3] Manasseh was elected an Associate of the Royal Academy in 1976, nominated by Ernö Goldfinger among others. In 1979 he became a full Academician, 'the nicest thing that's ever happened to me'.[4] In 1991 he was deputed – or, more likely, deputed himself – to convey in person the news of Paul Koralek's election as an

above 1989 Council and three past Presidents of the Royal West of England Academy, 1989, by Leonard Rosoman, showing Leonard Manasseh (foreground, left of centre).

Academician, for Koralek was a former student of his. Manasseh himself exhibited his own and his practice's work at the Royal Academy's Summer Exhibition – sometimes quite a lot of it – in every year that he was eligible to do so.

Manasseh designed the Royal Academy shop at Burlington House in 1982 with a mezzanine office floor on a diamond plan above the sales floor, reached by a spiral staircase – and, later, a 'Dada' T-shirt to sell in it. Throughout the 1970s and beyond, the partnership continued to work on a number of specialist, carefully worked out interiors. Geoffrey Scarsbrook in particular built up a continuous series of interior design projects at the partnership. From 1971 to 1972, he worked on a refit of the house of the Royal Society of Arts in John Adam Street in London. He followed this with two large projects, only one of which was executed – the surprisingly hard-surfaced interiors, in green and brown, for the British Council at its new headquarters in the Mall, designed to accommodate crowds of students.[5] The unbuilt project was a freestanding installation that the architects called the 'Space Rig'. Designed to exhibit small bronzes, ivories and alabasters in the eastern Cast Court of the Victoria and Albert Museum in South Kensington, it had been commissioned by the Director

above **The Royal Academy shop, London, in 1982.**

Roy Strong in the mid-1970s.[6] Some time later, in 1985–7, the practice refurbished and extended exhibition areas at the Old Royal Observatory at Greenwich for the Property Services Agency; the complex was opened by the celebrity astronomer Patrick Moore.[7] The partnership's last project of this type, for the same client, was the most dramatic of all: the remodelling of the Joseph E. Hotung Gallery of Oriental Antiquities at the British Museum in 1991–2. The walls of the gallery, in the Edward VII Galleries at the northern end of the site, were covered in gold leaf and the exhibits housed in glass showcases with minimal fixings. The result was 'a space that enhances the timelessness of the exhibits', wrote Penny McGuire in the *Architectural Review*. The partnership worked for a long time for the museum, building research laboratories for it and, in 1984, a new pair of entrance gates.

above **The proposed 'Space Rig' in the Cast Court of the Victoria and Albert Museum, London, mid-1970s.**

above top Visitor galleries at the Royal Obervatory, Greenwich, London, in 1985.
above The Joseph E. Hotung Gallery at the British Museum, London, opened in 1992.

The Leonard Manasseh Partnership

In 1981, the year in which Manasseh reached 65, the practice changed its name to the Leonard Manasseh Partnership, reflecting the greater role played by the other partners – Christopher Press and Geoffrey Scarsbrook – as well as the growing independence of other senior architects such as John Birkett-Smith. Although the office continued for about another ten years, and somewhat longer in Bath, it slowly reduced in size and eventually became a different type of practice. Yet the projects undertaken continued Manasseh and Baker's original themes right to the end.

In addition to the interior design schemes, the partnership continued to carry out characteristic infrastructure and landscaping projects. Birkett-Smith was for some time involved with a substantial project at Teignmouth, his perspective view appearing on the partnership's Christmas card for 1984. The scheme, which developed out of the previous projects for Foster Yeoman, was intended to provide a railway terminal along the edge of the water, but land was very limited; there was opposition locally to the dust and noise of the industrial processes that would have been involved; and the scheme required parliamentary approval. Together, these factors defeated the proposals. In the larger projects the partnership acted more as consultant designers than as architects, on occasion coming to the rescue when a developer's original scheme was rejected by the Royal Fine Art Commission (RFAC). This was how they came to design a series of striking interior and external features for Liverpool Central Station, acting alongside

above **The partnership's interiors at Liverpool Central Station, 1982.**

executive architects Edmund Percey Scherrer & Hicks (although they got top billing when the project was exhibited together with other urban-regeneration projects in Basle in 1983).[8] Likewise, Manasseh came to the rescue when Teignbridge District Council realised that it would require an outside designer for its new headquarters because of its sensitive setting alongside a Jacobean mansion in Newton Abbott in Devon.

above top Forde House, Newton Abbott, Devon.
above across to opposite page John Birkett-Smith's watercolour of the proposed new terminal at Teignmouth.

Manasseh himself designed the exterior of Forde House, successfully submitted the building to the RFAC, and obtained planning permission. From then on the council's Architects' Department took over the running of the job until its completion in 1987, somewhat spoiling it along the way, in Manasseh's opinion, with exposed services in the interior public areas.[9]

That year the partnership designed various power stations for the Central Electricity Generating Board (CEGB), including one for a site at Killingholme in north Lincolnshire. These projects comprised the modelling of massive overall shells, with colourful forms and strategically placed chimneys, which the CEGB varied in execution. Soon afterwards, however, the partnership designed a very large research station for British Gas to the west of Loughborough. Arranged around two large courtyards with ancillary buildings, it was faced in striped brick and aluminium,

above top **Killingholme Power Station, Lincolnshire, 1987.**

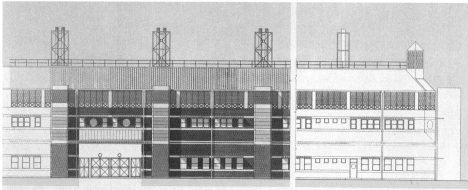

a further example of the architects styling a building designed by others and providing working drawings for the parts they were responsible for.[10] In this case, the commission came in after the Chairman of British Gas saw the partnership's work at the summer exhibition of the Royal Academy.[11] The concept design here was by Christopher Press, who at the same time also designed a large, unexecuted commercial project for the Bristol Royal Hotel site by the cathedral. The grandest of the partnership's clients remained faithful: Chesterton revised her Beaulieu plan in 1985, and two years later the Marquis of Hartington, with the Chatsworth Settlement, commissioned the partnership to design the New Cavendish Pavilion, a visitors' centre, by the River Wharfe north of his residence at Bolton Abbey. In the end, however, the existing pavilion was extended.

above top **British Gas Research Laboratories, Loughborough, Leicestershire, 1991: view.**
above **Detail of elevation.**

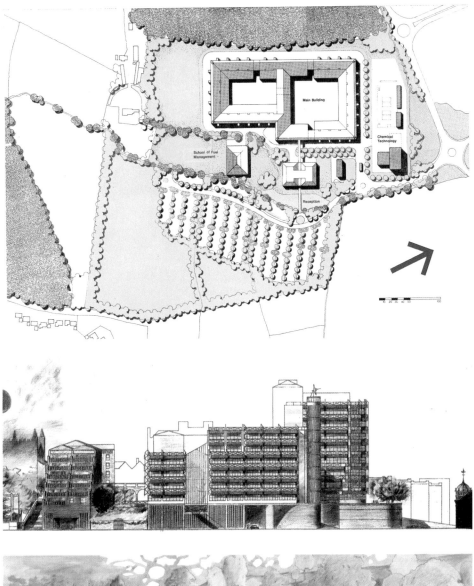

above top British Gas Research Laboratories: plan.
above middle Unexecuted scheme for the Royal Hotel site, Bristol, late 1980s.
above Ian Baker's design of 1986–7 for a new visitor pavilion at Bolton Abbey, North Yorkshire.

LMP Architects Ltd – the next generation

Neither Manasseh nor Baker ever really retired, but the partnership changed around them as they grew older. In 1984 their lease at Rathbone Street ended, and the landlords took over the building for themselves. The office transferred to 58 Bloomsbury Street, and, from 1987 until 1990, to its final London home in Store Street. After Jeremy Fry had bought the Freshford brewery in 1983, the Bath branch first camped out in the former Countess of Huntingdon's Chapel and then moved into a former bakery at 90 Walcot Street in the centre of the city; in 1987, Birkett-Smith left London to join it. This preceded the major reorganisation of 1994, when Manasseh and Baker retired as partners and became with Chesterton 'consultants' to the new Bath firm of LMP Architects Ltd, of which Birkett-Smith, Press and Stuart Ross became directors.[12]

The impetus for the reformed practice was a continuing supply of work for the Ministry of Defence, usually as the designers in a multi-disciplinary consortium headed by the engineering consultants Acer. In this role, the new firm designed much new accommodation at RAF Innsworth near Gloucester.[13] Other large projects included a major feasibility study for Castrol; however, even now the practice continued to specialise in planning for sensitive areas. The new office designed landscaping and kiosks as part of a remodelling of Kensington Palace Gardens and Palace Green, required for security reasons following the 1992 bomb attack on the Israeli Embassy there. They also designed an entry pavilion for Bristol Zoo, which opened in 1996,

above **Ian Baker's design for a visitors' pavilion on the Broad Walk, Kensington Gardens, London.**

winning a Civic Trust award and attracting the attention of the *RIBA Journal*.[14] That year Ross departed the company, and the remaining two directors left Walcot Street to work separately from offices in Frome and Trowbridge until the firm ceased trading in 2000. In the late 1990s Baker, from his London home, designed a visitors' pavilion and the 'Elfin Oak' enclosure at Kensington Gardens. He also designed an ambitious scheme for Regent's Park, of which only a small café was built. His final project, for a small octagonal timber visitors' shelter at Leeds Castle in Kent, was completed in 1998 – about the same time that Manasseh completed his home in Paziols. And thus, the partnership ended where it began: with designs for pavilions in gardens.

Baker spent his last years painting, right up to his death on 11 May 2010. Manasseh too has continued to paint and draw. In 2004, he exhibited his work at an exhibition entitled 'An Architect Ventures into Other Arts' at Lauderdale House in Highgate. And, as his *Who's Who* entry puts it, he is still 'being optimistic'. Nothing seems to shake it, he says.[15]

above left Sarah Manasseh's favourite portrait of Leonard, by John Donat, 2003.
above right Portrait head of Leonard Manasseh, by his sister Sylvia Manasseh, 1983.

above top Suburban Zebra, 1998, by Leonard Manasseh.
above Steam Engine, 2004, by Ian Baker.

Notes

1   *Independent*, 24 August 2002.
2   Manasseh and Partridge, letter to the *Architects'
    Journal*, 2 May 1979, p807; 'Manasseh: Outright
    Winner', *Architects' Journal*, 6 June 1979, p1152.
3   Leonard Manasseh, 'Architect Artists', *RIBA Journal*,
    May 1980, pp54–5. He discussed his collection
    in Catherine Croft, 'Lifelong Interests', *Building
    Design*, 17 February 2006, p20; and his painting in
    Manasseh BL interviews, Tape 9 Side A.
4   Manasseh BL interviews, Tape 7 Side B.
5   The building itself was designed by Howard V. Lobb
    and Partners.
6   Roy Strong, 'The Victoria and Albert Museum
    – 1978', *The Burlington Magazine*, May 1978,
    pp272–6.
7   Since remodelled by Allies and Morrison.
8   According to notes found in Manasseh's
    photographic archives. The station was remodelled
    in 2001 by the Owen Ellis Partnership.
9   Notes found in Manasseh's photographic archives;

Tim Borrett, Teignbridge District Council, email to
author 9 March 2010. The partnership competed
unsuccessfully for the design of a further local
authority headquarters, for Basingstoke and Deane,
in January 1985: Leonard Manasseh archives.
10 This project was carried out with a company called
    DGI International plc. Manasseh described the
    process in the Manasseh BL interviews, Tape 6
    Side A.
11 According to Stuart Ross (email, 16 March 2010).
    The Loughborough scheme itself was exhibited
    there in 1990.
12 This section was written following conversations
    with John Birkett-Smith (12 March 2010) and Stuart
    Ross (13 March 2010).
13 Now Imjin Barracks, and intended as the site for the
    headquarters of the NATO Allied Rapid Reaction
    Corps (ARRC).
14 *RIBA Journal*, July 1996, pp46–9.
15 Manasseh BL interviews, Tape 1 Side B.

above left **Ian Baker in 2008.**
above right **Leonard Manasseh, photographed by Morley von Sternberg in 2006.**

THE BRABAZON

6   Skyline

Leonard Manasseh, in the tradition of the Scandinavian architects who first impressed him in the 1940s, has remained resolutely silent about the intentions in his architecture and what the meaning of it might be. The closest he came to talking about any of these matters was in the course of his 1998 conversations with Louise Brodie for the 'Architects' Lives' project, the ellipses here conveying his moments of hesitancy in addressing the subject at all:

> I can't tell you what great architecture is. It's almost indefinable, I think ... but I believe that clients ought to be satisfied ... There has to be a dialogue and it's sometimes quite heated. But you actually learn from the dialogue, and you do things that you wouldn't have thought of doing before. And there's ... very often a happy compromise between you and your client, and so you're both happy. It's no good if neither of you are happy, and as far as I'm concerned it's no good if only the client is happy – then I haven't ... done a job that I'm proud of myself ... you've got to like what you do.
> Are you able to say what qualities you like to put in your designs?
> Well, I think the client's got to be happy. And you've got to try and satisfy him. And do your best to give him what he wants, and how he wants to live. What of course is helpful is that he doesn't really know, and it's lucky if what you tell him is what he wants. And that's how it's got to be. And so far I've had some fairly satisfied clients, who've really been quite pleased.[1]

As Paul Davies summarised when writing about the office in 1973, 'All the partners are distinctly suspicious of dogma in architecture.'[2]

A building that has no text to support it can explain itself by what it feels like to look at and be in, and sometimes too by the ideas that other designers have taken from it. It is not hard, for example, to see the family similarity between Manasseh's Brabazon Restaurant at Beaulieu and Sir Michael Hopkins's recent dining hall at Rice University in Texas – both strongly geometrical, big, cheerful, finely detailed, happily furnished and brightly lit spaces; or even between Manasseh's Rotork buildings and the many industrialised projects designed by his protégé's office. Hopkins, recalling the AA of the early 1960s, saw Manasseh as a 'proper, serious, modernist architect', but felt that the prevailing fashion, especially in housing design which was the major preoccupation of the period, was more literary and sociological than it was aesthetic. He points out, for example, that as a student influenced by Peter Smithson he doesn't remember drawing any elevations.[3] The 'Scandinavians', the 'Empiricists', and those who saw themselves as primarily concerned with designing life-assenting, attractive

opposite **The Brabazon Restaurant from the west.**

buildings were at a disadvantage in the era of what Alan Powers calls the 'new archi-tectural Calvinism' of the much louder Brutalists and their well-connected art-school allies, all proficient at writing and publishing.[4] However, the importance of the story of Leonard Manasseh does not rely on the attractive qualities of his buildings alone.

In the first place comes his refusal to be either an 'art boy' or a 'system boy', for example in his adoption of industrialised processes and components in the construction of buildings which were intended primarily to be fun to use and live in. The bright colours and the delicate details of his steel frames for façades and display cases alike show that there need not be any grand distinction between the technologists and the artists. The metonymic devices used in the partnership's buildings – the wheels, the struts, the canopies, the frames, the Euclidian geometry – not only illustrate how recent technology was seen and understood at the time, but also how architects related to it. Secondly, Manasseh's long association with the AA, which produced just about all his friends and professional connections, provides a chapter in the story of how British architecture developed after the Second World War which is quite different from the honed narratives of the Brutalists or Cedric Price and Archigram (for all of whom writing and publishing was so important). This alternative story was nevertheless more representative of much that was going on. Thirdly, the planning projects carried out with Elizabeth Chesterton describe a particular moment at the zenith of the post-war planning system, when England's traditionally dominant landowners allied with public authorities to create or protect parks and towns specifically for the enjoyment and education of the many. This was a heroic moment for a national planning vision that has been subsequently widely derided and largely dismantled. It was also a critical one in the development of the modern concept of heritage. And finally, the formal genres that Manasseh excelled in – exemplified by his projects for park and museum buildings, from the Festival bar to the structures at Beaulieu and the Wellington Country Park – are themselves part of a beautiful vision of life, of pavilions set among lawns and trees for resting and dining and having fun, derived perhaps from the Scandinavia that was portrayed in the wartime *Architectural Review*, but translated for an English audience.

And in some respects it is not a typically British temperament that predominates in this story. Elia Zenghelis, in time one of the founders of OMA, remembers that Manasseh cut quite a different figure from that of most of the teachers at the AA. Juries of students' work, he says, were in the late 1950s and early 1960s dominated by teachers who saw themselves as angry men, facing down and bullying intimidated students. When Manasseh came into the room the mood lightened: he tried to see things from the students' point of view; he was a very kind figure who sought to identify the strengths even of a weak scheme, and with his sense of humour he made people laugh.[5]

After some seven hours of interviews with Brodie, Manasseh finally ventured that an architect

> *cannot be a true architect unless he is involved with people ... because*
> *architecture without people is not in the end architecture ... it is*
> inextricably involved *with people, as far as I am concerned.*[6]

Peter Ahrends, remembering Manasseh's first-year class of 1951, says that what he found most appealing about Manasseh as a teacher was not only that he was a 'wonderful, unusually endearing man' but also his tremendous optimism – that he saw architecture as part of life, as a way of serving life better; that he taught him that architecture was about changing the world. It was, Ahrends said, this combination of humility and confidence that made him a beacon for the age.[7]

Notes

1   Manasseh BL interviews, Tape 4 Side B. The theme is reiterated in Tape 8 Side A.
2   Paul Davies, 'Profile of a Practice', *Architect*, August 1973, p49.
3   Author's conversation with Sir Michael Hopkins, 10 November 2009.
4   Alan Powers, *Britain*, London, Reaktion, 2007, p164.
5   Author's conversation with Elia Zenghelis, 12 March 2010.
6   Manasseh BL interviews, Tape 9 Side A.
7   Author's conversation with Peter Ahrends, 26 January 2010.

List of Works

Leonard Manasseh & Partners and its successor practices did not retain a complete set of job records, and consequently there is no full list of works with dates of commission or construction. This list has been compiled by putting facts together from all available sources. It does not include the many small commissions that the practice undertook.

The job numbers of the projects suggest that about 650 new files were opened between 1959 and the closure of LMP Architects Ltd in 2000. Dates in some cases have been approximated on the basis of the evidence available, but the general order has been determined by the job number where known. The date or dates given are the most accurate available to describe the period in which the project was conceived, designed and constructed, and the name of the job architect has been added where identified.

A double asterisk (**) indicates that the project has been demolished. A single asterisk (*) indicates that it has been drastically altered, sometimes beyond recognition.

Leonard Manasseh

1946

House Type A (police housing)
Designed as Assistant Architect, Hertfordshire County Council

1949–50

Maisonettes and Shops
Popple Way/Sish Lane, Stevenage, Hertfordshire
Designed as Senior Architect for Stevenage Development Corporation

1949–50

Luxury Restaurant, Festival of Britain (Unbuilt project)
Client: Festival of Britain Architecture Council

Architect & Building News, 13 January 1950, pp38–43
Builder, 13 January 1950, pp71–2
Architects' Journal, 26 January 1950, pp122–6
Building, February 1950, pp44–7
The Festival of Britain: Twentieth Century Society Journal 6, 2000, p71

opposite **The partnership's interior at Liverpool Central Station.**

Leonard Manasseh & Partners

1950–1

'51 Bar and service block**
Client: Festival of Britain Architecture
Council

Arena (Architectural Association journal), June
1964, p20
The Festival of Britain: Twentieth Century
Society Journal 6, 2000, pp 30, 71

1950

House
Pulborough, West Sussex
Client: Mr and Mrs Wright
Whereabouts of house unknown

1950–1

**Festival of Britain Land Travelling
Exhibition****
Client: Festival of Britain Architecture
Council
For chief designer Richard Levine, and in
association with other artists

Sadie Speight in association with Leonard Manasseh & Partners

1950–1

Rosie Lee Café**
Poplar, London
Client: Festival of Britain Architecture
Council

The Festival of Britain: Twentieth Century
Society Journal 6, 2000, p145

1950–1

Gay Kaye**
Handbag shop at 4 New Bond Street,
London
Client: Messrs Kaye
Job architect: Lois Hutchings

Architects' Journal, 3 January 1952, pp12–13
Bryan and Norman Westwood, *The Modern
Shop*, London, Architectural Press, 1952, p171

1950–1

Bowls Pavilion
Off Hilly Fields Crescent, Lewisham,
London
Client: London County Council

c.1951

The House of Richard**
Pen shop at 18 Liverpool Street, London
Client: Richard & Partners Ltd

Architects' Journal, 13 November 1952, p581

Leonard Manasseh & Partners

1951–3

Executive dining and ante-room**
Time and Life Building
153–7 New Bond Street, London
Client: Time and Life International
With Olive Sullivan

Architect & Building News, 5 March 1953,
pp281–96
Architects' Journal, 5 March 1953, pp305–18
Architectural Review, March 1953, pp156–72
Builder, 6 March 1953, pp373–9
Design (London), March 1953, pp11–55
Architectural Design, April 1953, pp89–112
Building, April 1953, pp130–7
Elain Harwood, *England: A Guide to Post-war*

Listed Buildings, London, Ellipsis, 2000,
section 8.6

1952–3

House

51 Campden Hill Road, Kensington,
London
Client: Mr and Mrs Philip Manasseh
Job architect: Bryan Field

Architect & Building News, 15 April 1954,
pp437–41
House & Garden, October 1954, pp72–3

1952

House in Highgate

(Apparently unbuilt project)
Client: unknown

Architectural Design, July 1953, p341

1953

House in North London

(Apparently unbuilt project)
Client: unknown

Architectural Design, July 1953, pp341–2

James Cubitt, Leonard Manasseh & Partners, Singapore

1954–6

4 terraced houses**

Off the Padang, Brunei Town (Bandar Seri
Begawan), Brunei
Client: The Sultan of Brunei

Leonard Manasseh & Partners

1955

Engineering works offices

Station Road, Kingswood, Bristol
Client: Frenchay Products Ltd (David Fry)
Job architect: Bryan Field

Architects' Journal, 26 July 1956, pp133–8
Architectural Design, December 1955, pp376–9
Trevor Dannatt, *Modern Architecture in Britain:
Selected Examples of Recent Building*, London,
Batsford, 1959, p66
Leonard Manasseh and Roger Cunliffe, *Office
Buildings*, London, Batsford, 1962, pp104–7

1955–6

La Reserve restaurant**

Gerrard Street, London
Client: La Reserve

Architectural Review, November 1956, pp 284,
335–8

1955–6

Electronics works offices**

Roebuck Road, Tolworth, Surrey
Client: Wayne Kerr

Architecture & Building (London), August 1956,
pp288–93

1957

Flats**

14 Ashburn Place, London
Client: Brian McDood [?]
Job architect: Bryan Field

*Survey of London, volume 42, Southern
Kensington*, London, Athlone Press/GLC, 1986,
p182

1957

Joinery works offices

Cowley, Middlesex

Client: Morgan & Partners

Exact whereabouts and present condition unknown

Wood, March 1958, pp84–5

c.1957

House

(Unexecuted project)

Hamble-le-Rice, Hampshire

Client: Peter Raymond

June Park, *House and Bungalows*, London, Batsford, pp177–9

House at Hamble-le-Rice, Hampshire, an unbuilt project from the late 1950s: east and south elevations.

1957–8

The Lawns*

South Grove, Highgate, London

Client: Mr and Mrs Peter Mack

Remodelled in 2000 by Eldridge Smerrin

Architect & Building News, 20 August 1958, pp268–72

Country Life, 31 January 2002, pp76–9

Bridget Cherry and Nikolaus Pevsner, *The Buildings of England, London 4: North*, London and New Haven, Yale UP, 2002, pp77, 408 and 416

Alan Powers, *The Twentieth Century House in Britain*, London, Aurum, 2004, pp186–9

RIBA Journal, July 2007, pp34–40

1957–9

House

6 Bacon's Lane, Highgate, London

Client: Leonard Manasseh and family

Job architect: Nicholas Quennell

Listed: Grade II*

Architectural Design, April 1961, pp159–62

House & Garden, March 1962, pp89–93

Alice Hope, *Town Houses*, London, Batsford, 1963, pp138–42.

Penelope Whiting, *New Houses*, London, Architectural Press, 1964, pp57–63

Arena (AA journal), June 1964, p19

Miranda H. Newton, *Architects' London Houses: The Homes of Thirty Architects since the 1930s*, London, Butterworth Architecture, 1992, pp32–7

Country Life, 25 January 2001, pp54–9

Bridget Cherry and Nikolaus Pevsner, *The Buildings of England, London 4: North*, London and New Haven, Yale UP, 2002, pp77 and 416

Alan Powers, *The Twentieth Century House in Britain*, London, Aurum, 2004, pp104–6

1957–60

Rutherford School

Penfold Street, Marylebone, London

Client: London County Council

Job architect: Bryan Field

Listed: Grade II*

Interbuild, June 1960, pp18–20

Official Architecture & Planning, September 1960, pp421–2

Architectural Review, November 1960, pp346–53

Architectural Design, December 1960, pp510–3

Arena (AA journal), June 1964, pp20–1

Jack Whitehead, 'The story of Marylebone Lower House, built as Rutherford School London NW1, in 1960' (undated typescript in former school library)

Research report, English Heritage, 1997

Elain Harwood, *England: A Guide to Post-war Listed Buildings*, London, Ellipsis, 2000, section 8.28

Bridget Cherry and Nikolaus Pevsner, *The Buildings of England, London 3: North West*, London and New Haven, Yale UP, 2002, p612

1958

Bossiney**

Eaton Park, Fairmile, Surrey

Client: unknown

June Park, *House and Bungalows*, London, Batsford, 1958, pp146–7, 151

Ian Nairn, *The Buildings of England, Surrey* (second edition, 1971), Harmondsworth, Penguin, p228

1959

House*

7 Bacon's Lane, Highgate, London

Client: Mr and Mrs Alfred Singer

Bridget Cherry and Nikolaus Pevsner, *The Buildings of England, London 4: North*, London and New Haven, Yale UP, 2002, pp77 and 416

Late 1950s–1976

Rotork Controls

Brassmill Lane, Bath

Client: Rotork Controls Ltd (Jeremy Fry)

Job architects for several phases included: Geoffrey Scarsbrook, Christopher Press

Architectural Review, November 1968, pp372–6

From late 1950s

RAF Housing

At various RAF bases around England

Client: Ministry of Defence

Job architect: Bryan Field

Late 1950s

Laboratories and offices**

Power Road, Chiswick, London

Client: Lautier Fils Ltd

Job architect: Bryan Field

Architecture & Building, June 1960, pp230–2

1960

Model motorway service station

Commissioned by the *Architectural Review*

Architectural Review, December 1960, pp407–19

1960–1

Hampstead Civic Trust improvement scheme*

Hampstead High Street, London

With Elizabeth Chesterton. Job architect: David Etherton

Early 1960s

Refinery offices, laboratories and canteen

Mersin [?], Turkey

Client: ATAS

Condition unknown

Early 1960s–mid-1960s

Gospel hall and classrooms*

439 Oldfield Lane North, Greenford, Middlesex

Client: Greenford Gospel Church

Job architect: Bryan Field

1960–5

Furzedown Teachers' Training College
Welham Road, Streatham, London
Client: London County Council
Job architects: Bryan Field, Donald Meyer
and Jenny Wolton

Architectural Review, January 1961, p19
Architects' Journal, 26 June 1963, pp1335–8
Concrete & Constructional Engineering, March
1964, pp92–6
Arena (AA journal), June 1964, p21
Architectural Review, May 1965, pp336–42
Architect & Building News, 7 July 1965, pp17–24
Bridget Cherry and Nikolaus Pevsner, *The
Buildings of England, London 2: South*, London
and New Haven, Yale UP, 2002, p698.

1962–4

House
(Unexecuted project)
La Vigie, near St Tropez, France
Client: Mike Behrens

Arena (AA journal), June 1964, p22

1962–6

Dodson Street Estate
Waterloo, London
Client: London County Council/Greater
London Council
Job architect and designer: John Roberts

1962–5

House
3 Bank Lane, Roehampton, London
Client: Mr and Mrs Peter Rea
Job architect: Geoffrey Scarsbrook

1962

Garth Castle restoration and conversion*
Near Keltneyburn, Perthshire
Client: David Fry
Job architect: John Roberts

Ideal Home, May 1965, pp68–71
Mary and Neville Ward, *Living Rooms*, London,
Macdonald & Co, 1970, pp2–3

1962–6

Gilbert Murray Hall of Residence
Manor Road, Oadby, Leicestershire
Client: University of Leicester
Principal job architect: Robert Huddleston,
assisted by Michael Hopkins
Warden's house designer and job architect:
Robert Huddleston

Nikolaus Pevsner, Elizabeth Williamson
with Geoffrey K. Brandwood, *The Buildings
of England, Leicestershire and Rutland*,
Harmondsworth, Penguin, 1984, pp47 and 340
Robert Huddleston, *Thundertoes: An
Autobiography*, Bristol, Redcliffe Press, 2009,
pp140–54

1963–8

Brockles Mead Estate
Harlow, Essex
Client: Harlow Development Corporation
Job architects included: Christopher
Press

Architectural Review, July 1966, p45
James Bettley and Nikolaus Pevsner, *The
Buildings of England, Essex*, London and New
Haven, Yale UP, 2007, p463

1964

Electronics works and offices

Durban Road, Bognor Regis, West Sussex
Client: Wayne Kerr Ltd
Designer and job architect: Robert
Huddleston
Current condition unknown

Robert Huddleston, *Thundertoes: An
Autobiography*, Bristol, Redcliffe Press, 2009,
pp140–54

1964–7

Drum House**

River Lane, Petersham, Surrey
Client: Mr and Mrs Christopher Carr Jones
Job architects: Robert Huddleston, Anne
Behrend

Ian Nairn, *The Buildings of England, Surrey*
(second edition, 1971), Harmondsworth,
Penguin, pp78 and 411
House & Garden, May 1976, pp126–9
Bridget Cherry and Nikolaus Pevsner, *The
Buildings of England, London 2: South*, London
and New Haven, Yale UP, 2002, pp92, 466 and
515–16
Robert Huddleston, *Thundertoes: An
Autobiography*, Bristol, Redcliffe Press, 2009,
pp140–54

1964–7

Courtyards

River Lane, Petersham, Surrey
Client: Mr and Mrs Richard Lester
Job architects: Robert Huddleston, Nigel
Woolner and Alan Ayling

June Park, *Houses for Today*, London, Batsford,
1971, pp15–18
Ian Nairn, *The Buildings of England: Surrey*
(second edition, 1971), Harmondsworth,
Penguin, pp78, 411

House & Garden, May 1976, pp128–9
Bridget Cherry and Nikolaus Pevsner, *The
Buildings of England, London 2: South*, London
and New Haven, Yale UP, 2002, pp92, 466,
515–16
Robert Huddleston, *Thundertoes: An
Autobiography*, Bristol, Redcliffe Press, 2009,
pp140–54

1964–5

Belvedere restaurant**

Holland Park, Kensington, London
Client: J. Lyons & Co
Job architects: Geoffrey Scarsbrook and
Nigel Woolner

1964

Hook Line and Sinker restaurant**

73 Baker Street, London
Client: J. Lyons & Co
Job architects: Geoffrey Scarsbrook and
John Roberts

1964–70

Office conversion*

Freshford brewery, Freshford, Bath
Client: Leonard Manasseh and Partners
Job architect: Christopher Press
Architectural Review, May 1972, pp290–9

1965–8

Steeplehall Estate

Pitsea, Basildon, Essex
Client: Basildon Development Corporation
Job architect: Bryan Field

c.1965

Language laboratories [?]
University of Leicester
Client: University of Leicester
Situation unknown

c.1965

House*
73B Castlenau, Barnes, London
Client: Mr and Mrs Norman Clogg

1965–6

Housing
Riverside Close, Bridge, Kent
Client: Chris Beale
Designer and job architect: Robert
Huddleston, assisted by Christopher
Press

John Newman, *The Buildings of England, Kent
and North East Kent*, Harmondsworth, Penguin,
1983, pp121 and 160.
Robert Huddleston, *Thundertoes: an autobiography*, Bristol, Redcliffe Press, 2009, pp 140–54

1966

House
Brickwheat Bottom, near Winterborne
Whitechurch, Blandford Forum, Dorset
Client: Mr and Mrs J. Craven

1966–81

King's Lynn Law Courts
South Quay, King's Lynn, Norfolk
Client: Norfolk County Council
Job architect: Tony Thompson

Architects' Journal, 18 November 1964,
pp1160–2
RIBA Journal, March 1981, p55

Nikolaus Pevsner and Bill Wilson, *The Buildings
of England, Norfolk 2: North-West & South*,
London, Penguin, 1999, pp167 and 484

1966–8

Lane's End warden's house*
Beaford, Devon
Client: The Dartington Hall Trust
Job architects: Geoffrey Scarsbrook and
John Thake

1966–7

Looking Glass Restaurant**
Royal Lancaster Hotel, Bayswater Road,
London
Client: Rank Organisation
Job architect: Geoffrey Scarsbrook

The Architects' Journal (ed.), *Principles of Hotel
Design*, London, Architectural Press, 1970, pp35
and 60

c.1966

Giffords
Hadlow Down, East Sussex
Client: Chris Beale
Designer and job architect: Robert
Huddleston. Altered but restored in the
1990s by Robert Huddleston to the original
design.

Robert Huddleston, *Thundertoes: An
Autobiography*, Bristol, Redcliffe Press, 2009,
pp140–54

1966

Houses
26–30 Grange Road, Highgate, London
Client: Esther Manasseh
Job architect: John Roberts

1967

Old people's housing

Parkhurst Road, Pitsea, Essex
Client: Basildon Development Corporation
Job architects: Bryan Field and Donald
Meyer
Ministry of Housing Award for Good Design,
South-east (northern) region (lower density
public sector)

Architects' Journal, 16 December 1970, p1437
James Bettley and Nikolaus Pevsner, *The
Buildings of England, Essex*, London and New
Haven, Yale UP, 2007, p122

1967–72

Hunters Moon housing

Dartington, Devon
Client: The Dartington Hall Trust
Job architect: Christopher Press

Bridget Cherry and Nikolaus Pevsner, *The
Buildings of England, Devon*, Harmondsworth,
Penguin, 1989, pp114, 315 and 319

1967

The Lighthouse

House at North Road Sandwich Bay, Kent
Client: Mr Breeden
Job architect, original house: John Thake
Job architect, extension (c.1973): Alex
Billeter

1967–74

Beaulieu: National Motor Museum and visitors' facilities

Beaulieu, Hampshire
Clients: Beaulieu Museum Trust, Beaulieu
Estate and Montagu Ventures Ltd
Job architects included: Christopher Hulls,
Christopher Press and John Thake

RIBA Southern Region Award 1973
Structural Steel Design Award 1974
National Heritage 'Museum of the Year' Award
1974
RICS and *The Times* Conservation Award (third
prize) 1975

Architect & Building News, 23 November 1966,
p895
Design (London), February 1972, pp48–9
Building Design, 7 July 1972, p13
Building, 4 August 1972, pp28–34
Architectural Design, August 1972, pp475–6
Design (London), October 1972, pp33–9
Tubular Structures, October 1972, pp17–20
Architectural Review, December 1972, pp324–38
Architectural Forum, March 1973, p16
Architecture Plus, March 1973, p11
Arkitekten (Copenhagen), 7 June 1973, pp196–9
Domus, June 1973, p18
A&U, July 1973, pp115–22
Brick Bulletin, July 1973, pp16–17
Architecture d'Aujourd'hui, July/August 1973,
pp22–5
Bauen & Wohnen, October 1973, pp405–8 and
417
Architects' Journal, 20 November 1974,
pp1188–9
Detail, January/February 1975, pp69–72
Landscape Design, November 1978, pp29–32

1967–72

Arden Estate extension

Hoxton Street/Pitfield Street/Myrtle Walk,
Hoxton, London
Client: Greater London Council
Job architects: Bryan Field and John Thake

c.1967–9

Shrewsbury Gospel Hall

Stracey Road, Harlesden, London
Job architects: Bryan Field and John Thake

1969–72

Royal Society of Arts remodelling
8 John Adam Street, London
Client: Royal Society of Arts
Job architect: Geoffrey Scarsbrook

Journal of the Royal Society of Arts, February
1972, pp133–6
Simon Bradley and Nikolaus Pevsner, *The
Buildings of England, London 6: Westminster*,
London and New Haven, Yale UP, 2003, p328

1969–71

Fellows' houses
Pearce's Yard, Grantchester,
Cambridgeshire
Client: King's College, Cambridge;
Cambridge University Estate Management
Advisory Service
Job architect: John Thake

1969–1974

Wellington Country Park
Stratfield Saye, Berkshire
Client: Stratfield Saye Estates Management
Co Ltd
Job architect: John Thake

European Architectural Heritage Year Award
1975
RICS and *The Times* Conservation Awards
(second prize) 1975.

Architects' Journal, 24 July 1974, pp191–2
Building, 26 July 1974, p66
Architectural Review, August 1975,
pp92–7
Building Specification, September 1975, pp23–5
Landscape Design, November 1978, pp33–5

c.1969–76

**New buildings at Hedingham County
Secondary School**
Client: Essex County Education Authority
Designers and job architects: Geoffrey
Scarsbrook and Alex Billeter

Early 1970s–1975

British Council interiors
10 Spring Gardens, London
Client: British Council
Job architect: Geoffrey Scarsbrook

Architect (London), April 1975, p36
RIBA Journal, November 1976, p461
Design (London), March 1977, pp52–3

Early 1970s–1975

Snowdon visitors' centre
(Unbuilt scheme)
Client: Countryside Commission
Architects' Journal, 23 July 1975, pp172–5

Early 1970s–1980

Theale Depot
Wigmore Lane, Theale, Berkshire
Client: Foster Yeoman Ltd
Job architect: John Birkett-Smith

1971–4

Canbury Park Gospel Hall extension
234A Canbury Park Road, Kingston-upon-
Thames, Surrey
Client: Canbury Park Church
Job architect: Bryan Field

Early 1970s–1974

House*
55 Lower Radley, Abingdon, Oxfordshire
(then Berkshire)
Client: John and Lou Curtis
Job architect: Christopher Press

Early 1970s–1974

Bath Law Courts
(Unbuilt project)
Client: Bath City Council

Architects' Journal, 7 August 1974, pp304–8
Building, 9 August 1974, p37
Architects' Journal, 21 August 1974, p425
Architect (London), October 1974, pp51 and 59
Building Design, 25 October 1974, p3

Early 1970s

House remodelling
1 Queen's Parade, Bath
Client: Joy Fry

1975

New kitchens and common rooms
Magdalen College, Oxford
(Competition entry, runner up)
Client: Magdalen College, Oxford
Project architect: Nigel Honer

Architects' Journal, 7 May 1975, pp970–4

Mid-1970s

Zoo master plan and structures
Port Lympne Wild Animal Park, Aldington
Road, Lympne, Kent
Client: John Aspinall

The Elephant House at Port Lympne Wild Animal
Park, mid-1970s.

1975–7

Royal Mews, Windsor
Client: Property Services Agency
Job architect: John Birkett-Smith

Mid-1970s

Eastfield Road housing
Westbury-on-Trym, Bristol
Client: City of Bristol
Job architect: Christopher Press

1977

Torr Quarry
East Cranmore, near Shepton Mallet,
Somerset
Client: Foster Yeoman Ltd
Job architects included: Christopher Press,
Bryan Field

Architects' Journal, 14 June 1978, pp1149–50

1977

Barristers' chambers

(Unbuilt project)
Niblet Hall, Inner Temple, London
Client: The Honourable Society of the Inner
Temple
Architectural Review, January 1978, p39

Leonard Manasseh's drawing of the partnership's
scheme for Niblet Hall, Inner Temple.

1979

Courthouse, Trinidad

(Unsuccessful competition entry)
Architects' Journal, 18 April 1979, pp789–91

Late 1970s–1980s

Marina

(Unexecuted project)
The Crumbles, Eastbourne, East Sussex
Client: Trustees of the Chatsworth
Settlement

c.1978

'Space Rig'

(Unbuilt project)
Victoria and Albert Museum, Brompton
Road, London
Designer: Alex Billeter

1979–1982

Radipole Lake Pumping Station

Client: Weymouth & Portland District
Council, agents for Wessex Water
Job architect: Stuart Ross
RIBA Journal, March 1981, p61

1970s–1980s

House

Champeau, near Merindol, France
Client: Leonard Manasseh and family
Job architect: John Roberts
RIBA Journal, February 1980, p41
International Asbestos Cement Review (AC),
July 1981, pp52–3

Late 1970s

Waterloo Road housing

Southwark, London
Client: Greater London Council
Job architect: John Batstone

c.1980

Perrett House sheltered housing

Redcross Street, Old Market, Bristol
Client: Bristol Municipal Charities
Job architects: Christopher Press and
Stuart Ross

Leonard Manasseh Partnership

Early 1980s

Master plan, classrooms and dormitories*
Hordle House School
Milford-on-Sea, Hampshire
Client: Hordle House School Trust

c.1980–1982

Liverpool Central Station**
Ranelagh Street, Liverpool
Client: Viking Property Group
Architectural treatment, with Edmund
Percey Scherrer & Hicks

New Development in Historic Towns (Exhibition
catalogue), Basle, Gewerbemuseum Basle, 1983,
pp26–7

1982–6

Glensanda 'superquarry'
On Loch Linnhe, Argyllshire
Client: Yeoman (Morvern) Ltd

1982–7

Forde House
Newton Abbott, Devon
Client: Teignbridge District Council
Architectural treatment, for Teignbridge
Architects' Department

Bridget Cherry and Nikolaus Pevsner, *The
Buildings of England, Devon*, Harmondsworth,
Penguin, 1989, p591

1982

Royal Academy Shop**
Burlington House, Piccadilly, London
Client: Royal Academy
Job architect: Donald Meyer

1982–6

**Kingston Lacy master plan and
landscaping**
Kingston Lacy, near Wimborne Minster,
Dorset
Client: National Trust
Job architect: John Birkett-Smith

1983–4

**Western Quay extension and bulk
cargo facilities**
(Unbuilt project)
Teignmouth, Devon
Client: Teignmouth Quay Company Ltd
Job architect: John Birkett-Smith

1983–4

House conversion
Freshford brewery, Freshford, Bath
Client: Jeremy Fry
Job architect: Christopher Press

Vogue, November 1988, pp208–13

1984–5

Elderly persons' housing
Redcross Mews, Old Market, Bristol
Client: Bristol Municipal Charities
Job architects: Christopher Press and
Stuart Ross

1985–7

Exhibition gallery and visitor facilities*
Royal Observatory, Greenwich, London
Client: Property Services Agency Museums
and Galleries Group
Construction (London), September 1987, pp23–4

Late 1980s

Royal Hotel site development
(Unbuilt project)
College Green, Bristol
Client: Beazer Estates
Job architect: Christopher Press

1986–7

New Cavendish Pavilion
(Unbuilt project)
Bolton Abbey, North Yorkshire
Client: The Trustees of the Chatsworth
Settlement

1987

Model power stations
(Unbuilt projects)
With Derek Latham and Associates,
landscape architects
Killingholme, Lincolnshire, and other sites
Client: Central Electricity Generating
Board

c.1990

Technical centre
(Unbuilt project)
Swindon, Wiltshire
Client: Burmah Castrol
Job architect: Christopher Press

1989–91

British Gas Research Centre
Holywell Park, Loughborough,
Leicestershire
Client: British Gas
Architectural treatment, with DGI
International plc
Designer and job architect: Christopher
Press
Building Design, 25 June 1993, p22

1990–2

Joseph E. Hotung Gallery
British Museum, London
Client: Property Services Agency Museums
and Galleries Group
Job architect: Nick Thompson
Building, 4 December 1992, pp56–8
Architectural Review, April 1993, pp82–3

1990–2

Park staff compound
Hampstead Heath (off Highgate Road),
London
Client: Corporation of City of London
Job architect: Phin Manasseh
Building, 30 July 1993, pp25–8

LMP Architects Ltd

1990s

**Personnel and Training Command
accommodation**
RAF Innsworth, Gloucestershire
Client: Ministry of Defence

1990s

Projects at Larkhill, Windsor, Yeovilton, Culdrose and Portland military bases
Client: Ministry of Defence

1990s

Entrance pavilion and animal enclosure, Bristol Zoo
Clifton, Bristol
Client: Bristol Zoological Society
Job architect: Christopher Press

Civic Trust Award

RIBA Journal, July 1996, pp46–9

1992–9

Landscaping and kiosks
Palace Green, Kensington Palace Gardens, London
Client: Crown Estate

c.1997

Elfin Oak Enclosure and visitors' pavilion
Kensington Gardens, London
Client: Royal Parks

Late 1990s

Boat House Café
(Partial execution of larger scheme)
Regent's Park, London
Client: Royal Parks

Late 1990s

Various water/sewage treatment works
Client: Severn Trent

1997–8

Wykeham Martin Centre
Leeds Castle, near Maidstone, Kent
Client: Leeds Castle

Leonard Manasseh

1998

House
Paziols, near Perpignan, France
Client: Leonard Manasseh and family

Bibliography

Books including entries on buildings by Leonard Manasseh & Partners

The Architects' Journal (ed.), *Principles of Hotel Design*, London, Architectural Press, 1970, pp35 and 60.

Trevor Dannatt, *Modern Architecture in Britain: Selected Examples of Recent Building*, London, Batsford, 1959, p66.

Alice Hope, *Town Houses*, London, Batsford, 1963, pp138–42.

Leonard Manasseh and Roger Cunliffe, *Office Buildings*, London, Batsford, 1962, pp104–7.

Miranda H. Newton, *Architects' London Houses: The Homes of Thirty Architects since the 1930s*, London, Butterworth Architecture, 1992, pp32–7.

June Park, *Houses and Bungalows*, London, Batsford, 1958, pp 146–7, 151 and 177–9.

June Park, *Houses for Today*, London, Batsford, 1971, pp115–18.

Mary and Neville Ward, *Living Rooms*, London, Macdonald & Co, 1970, pp2–3.

Bryan and Norman Westwood, *The Modern Shop*, London, Architectural Press, 1952, p171.

Penelope Whiting, *New Houses*, London, Architectural Press, 1964, pp57–63.

Published texts on Leonard Manasseh and his office

'AA president 1964–65: Leonard Manasseh', *Arena* (AA journal), June 1964, pp19–22.

Paul Davies, 'Profile of a practice: 8. Leonard Manasseh & Partners', *Architect* (London), August 1973, pp48–50.

'RIBA: Manasseh outright winner in RIBA council election', *Architects' Journal*, 6 June 1979, p1152.

Catherine Croft, 'Lifelong Collections', *Building Design*, 17 February 2006, p20.

Timothy Brittain-Catlin, 'Ian Baker' (obituary), *Guardian*, 21 May 2010.

Published texts by Leonard Manasseh

'A House at Sonning', *Architectural Association Journal*, January 1943, pp54–6.

'time, trees and architecture' (with Stefan Buzás), *Architectural Review*, August 1943, p52.

Office Buildings (with Roger Cunliffe), London, Batsford, 1962.

'Presidential Address: the Moment of Truth', *Arena* (AA journal), November 1964, pp95–102.

The Historic Core of King's Lynn: A Study and Plan (in association with Elizabeth Chesterton), London, 1964.

Snowdon Summit: A Report (in association with Elizabeth Chesterton), London, Countryside Commission, 1975.

'Enid Caldicott: In Memoriam' (memorial

opposite **The Joseph E. Hotung Gallery at the British Museum, London, opened in 1992.**

address), *Architectural Association Quarterly*, no 3, 1978, pp60–1.

'Hurrah for Architecture!' (letter, with John Partridge), *Architects' Journal*, 2 May 1979, p807.

'Eric Lyons: fought for good architecture' (obituary), *Architects' Journal*, 27 February 1980, p419.

'Low-Pitched Revival', *RIBA Journal*, February 1980, p41.

'Societies for architect-artists, illustrators and sculptors: Architect Artists', *RIBA Journal*, May 1980, pp54–5.

'Le Corbusier lives on', *RIBA Journal*, June 1981, pp12–13.

'The thirties remembered. "Look, stranger, at this island now" – English architectural drawings of the 1930s' (exhibition review), *AA files*, no 4, July 1983, pp96–101.

'The taming of technology' (review of 151 Rosebery Avenue, London, by Troughton McAslan), *Architecture Today*, May 1992, pp30–2 and 35.

President's Choice: An Exhibition of Architecture in the 150th Anniversary Year (exhibition catalogue), Bristol, Royal West of England Academy, 1994.

'Philip Powell 1921–2003' (obituary), *Architectural Review*, July 2003, p17.

Interviews

Elizabeth Chesterton interviewed by Louise Brodie, 1997, 'Architects' Lives', British Library Sound Archive, reference C467/25 (recorded October 1997).

Leonard Manasseh interviewed by Louise Brodie, 1998, 'Architects' Lives', British Library Sound Archive, reference C467/27 (recorded January–March 1998).

Index

Note: page numbers in italics refer to illustrations.

Acer 130
Ahrends, Peter 5, 137
Alcan 104
Amsterdam School 60
apartment buildings 34, 63, *64*
Architectural Association (AA) 3–4, 5, 7–8, 42, 136
Arden Estate extension, Hoxton 70–2, *70*, *71*
Ashburn Place flats 34, 141
Aslin, C. H. 8
Asplund, Erik Gunnar 5
awards 68, 109–10, 116, 131

Bacon's Lane, Highgate 25–8, *25*, *26*, *27*, *28*, *29*, 142, 143
Baker, Ian 18–22
   Bolton Abbey visitors' pavilion (unbuilt) *129*
   Broad Walk, Kensington Gardens, visitors' pavilion *130*
   Fellows' houses for King's College, Cambridge *35*
   Furzedown Teachers' Training College 54–5, 58
   images of *18*, *21*, 73, *86*, *133*
   Kensington Gardens 131
   King's Lynn Law Courts *91*, 92
   Leeds Castle visitors' shelter 131
   National Motor Museum *86*, *99*, 100, *101*
   paintings and drawings 19–20, 77, 131, *132*
   in partnership with Leonard Manasseh 16, 21, 73, *73*, 79
   private housing projects 34, *35*, 39
   public housing projects 68, 74
   retirement 130, *133*
   Rotork works 37
   Snowdon scheme 93
   Torr Quarry 94
Baker, Patricia 21
Bank Lane, Roehampton 28–9, *29*, 30, 144

Basildon New Town 66–8, 145
Bath, Queen's Parade, private house 40, 149
Bath Law Courts (unbuilt) 80–3, *81*, *82*, *83*, 149
Bath office 77, *78*, 130
Bath Preservation Trust 82
Beaford, Lane's End 32, 146
Behrens, Mike, house (unbuilt) 32–3, *33*
Bell, Susan 89–90, 93
Belvedere restaurant, Holland Park 44, 145
Billeter, Alex 76–7, 92
Birkett-Smith, John 76
   Eastbourne Marina 113
   Kingston Lacy Estate 119
   Leonard Manasseh Partnership 125
   LMP Architects Ltd 130, 131
   National Motor Museum 100
   Teignmouth terminal (unbuilt) *126–7*
Birling Gap scheme 112
Black, Misha 10
Bloch, Alex 77
Bognor Regis, Wayne Kerr headquarters 43, *43*, 141, 145
Bolton Abbey visitor pavilion (unbuilt) 128, *129*, 152
bowls pavilion, Lewisham 16, *17*, 140
Brabazon restaurant 104, *105*, *106*, *134*
Brennan, Dennis 109
Brickwheat Bottom, private house 32, *32*, 146
Bridge, Riverside Close 34, 146
Bristol
   housing projects 77, 149, 151
   Old Market area 93
   Royal Hotel scheme (unbuilt) 128, *129*, 152
   Zoo 130–1, 153
British Council headquarters scheme 122, 148
British Gas Research Laboratories 127–8, *128*, *129*, 152
British Museum schemes 123, *124*, 152
Brockles Mead, Harlow 62–4, *62*, *63*, *64*, *65*, 144

Brodie, Louise 135
Brookes, John 31
Brown, Eric 4
Brunei project 21, 141
Burford House 75–6
Burton, Richard 5
Buzás, Stefan 3, 4, 5, 9, 21

Campden Hill Road, Kensington, private
    house 23–4, 23, 141
Canbury Park Gospel Hall 74, 148
Capon, Kenneth 24
Caröe, Martin 119
Caroe and Partners 119
Carr Jones family, house 30
Casson, Hugh 10, 15, 16, 99, 102
Castlenau, Barnes, private house 34, 146
Central Electricity Generating Board (CEGB)
    127
Champeau, Provence, holiday home 33, 34,
    150
Charlotte Street office 53
Chatsworth Settlement 112, 128
Chesterton, Elizabeth 87–90, 88
    King's Lynn scheme 90–2
    Kingston Lacy Estate 119, 120
    LMP Architects Ltd 130
    National Motor Museum 96, 98–100, 105,
        128
    other planning-led projects 111, 112–13
    public roles 119
    Snowdon scheme 93
    Torr Quarry 94
Chesterton, Maurice 87
Chippenham town centre 92–3
Civic Trust
    award 131
    Hampstead improvement scheme 88
Colvin, Brenda 90
competitions 4, 9–10, 92
Countryside Commission 93, 113, 116
Courtyards, Petersham 30, 31
Cox, Anthony 3, 8, 25
Craven family, house 32, 32
Cubitt, James 3, 21, 141
Cunliffe, Clemency 53
Cunliffe, Roger 53, 73
Curtis, John and Lou, private house 31

Dalwood, Hubert 47
Darbourne & Darke 69
Dartington
    Hunters Moon Estate 77, 112, 112, 147
    planning schemes 98, 112
Dartington Hall Trust 32, 111
de Klerk, Michel 60
Derek Lovejoy & Partners 105
design language 41–2, 79, 135–6
Dodson Street Estate 32, 68–70, 69, 144
Donat, John 131
Dower, Michael 111
Drum House, Petersham 30–1, 30, 145
Dudok, Willem Marinus 60, 72
Dyson, James 35, 37

Eastbourne Marina 113, 113, 150
Edmund Percey Scherrer & Hicks 126
educational projects 46–9, 53–61, 77, 151
Elias, David 3
Elias, Esther see Manasseh, Esther (mother of
    Leonard)
Elias, Joseph 3, 10
Etherton, David 79
European Architectural Heritage Year Award
    116

Farrell/Grimshaw Partnership 37
Feilden, Richard 77
Felix J. Samuely and Partners 37, 101
Feock boathouse 40
Fergusson, Adam 81
Festival of Britain projects 9–10, 9, 13–15, 13,
    14, 139–40
Field, Bryan 74
Finchley, National Westminster Bank 76
Forde House, Newton Abbott 118, 126–7, 151
Foster, Norman 31
Foster Yeoman 94, 95, 125
Frenchay works 36–7, 36, 74, 141
Freshford brewery 78
    house conversion 39, 40, 151
    office conversion 77, 79, 145
Fry, David 35, 37, 39
Fry, Jeremy 35–6, 36, 37, 39, 40
Fry, Joy, private house 40
Furzedown Teachers' Training College 52,
    53–8, 54, 55, 56, 57, 144

Garth Castle 39–40, *41*, 144
Gavin, A. 18
Gay Kaye handbag shop 15–16, *16*, 140
Gibberd, Frederick 15, 61–2
Gilbert Murray Hall 58–61, *59*, *60*, 144
Glass, Ruth 88
GLC housing 69–72
Glensanda Quarry 96, 151
Goldfinger, Ernö 121
Grantchester, Pearce's Yard 34, *35*, 148
Greater London Council, housing 69–72
Greenford Gospel Church 74, 143
Greenwich Royal Observatory 123, *124*, 152
Gruffydd, J. St Bodfan 105
Guy Morgan & Partners 4

Hampstead Civic Trust improvement scheme
    88, 143
Hampstead Heath, staff compound *116*, 117,
    152
Harlesden, Shrewsbury Gospel Hall *75*, 147
Harlow New Town 61–4, 144
Hayward, Joe 44
Hedingham County Secondary School 77, *78*,
    148
Henrion, Hardy, statue by 29, *133*
Hertfordshire County Council 8
Highgate houses 24–30, 141, 142
Hodgkinson, Patrick 74
Holford, William 88
Holland Park, Belvedere restaurant 44, 145
Holliday, Clifford 9
Hook Line and Sinker 44, *44*, *45*, 145
Hopkins, Michael 61, 89, 135
Hordle House School 151
House of Richard *17*, 140
housing 34, 61–72, 77
    see also private houses
Hoxton estate 70–2, *70*, *71*, 147
Hubbard, Brian 96, 100
Huddleston, Robert 34
Hulls, Christopher 73–4, 100
Hunters Moon Estate 77, 112, *112*, 147

industrial buildings 36–9, 43, 94–6, 127–8
Inner Temple, Niblet Hall 150, *150*
Inskip, Peter 119
interior design projects 43–4, 122–4

J. Lyons restaurants 44, *44*, 145
James Cubitt, Leonard Manasseh & Partners,
    Singapore 21, 141
Jarrett, E. R. 18
Johnson-Marshall, Stirrat 8
Jordan, Robert Furneaux 3, 10
Joseph E. Hotung Gallery 123, *124*, 152

Kelly, Mike 84
Kelly, Rhoda 72, 73
Kensington, Campden Hill Road, private
    house 23–4, *23*, 141
Kensington Gardens visitors' pavilion *130*, 131,
    153
Kensington Palace Gardens 130, 153
Killingholme Power Station 127, *127*, 152
King Solomon Academy 49
King's College, Cambridge 34, *35*, 148
King's Lynn Law Courts *91*, 92, *92*, 146
King's Lynn project 90–2
Kingston Lacy Estate 119, *120*, 151
Kingston School of Art 4
Koralek, Paul 5, 121–2
Kramer, Piet 60

La Reserve restaurant 43, 141
La Vigie 32–3, *33*, 144
Lane's End, Beaford 32, 146
Lansbury Estate 15
Lasdun, Denys 61
Lautier Fils Ltd 74, 143
law courts, Bath 80–3, *81*, *82*, *83*
Lawns, The, Highgate, private house 24–5, *25*,
    142
LCC *see* London County Council (LCC)
Le Corbusier 21–2, 24, 58
Leeds Castle visitors' shelter 131, 153
Leicester, Gilbert Murray Hall 58–61, *59*, *60*,
    144
Leonard Manasseh Partnership 125, 130,
    151–2
Lester, Richard, private house 30
Lewisham, bowls pavilion 16, *17*, 140
Lighthouse, Sandwich Bay 32, *33*, 77
Lillington Gardens Estate, Pimlico 69
Liverpool Central Station 125–6, *125*, *138*, 151
LMP Architects Ltd 130–1, 152–3
Lock, Max 90

London County Council (LCC)
    bowls pavilion, Lewisham 16
    Furzedown Teachers' Training College
        53–8
    housing 68–70
    Rutherford School 46–9
Looking Glass restaurant 44, *45*, 146
Lower Radley, private house 31–2, *31*, 149

Magdalen College, kitchens and common
        rooms (unbuilt) 92, 149
Maisons Jaoul 24
Manasseh, Esther (mother of Leonard) 1, 3, 30
Manasseh, Karin (first wife of Leonard) 9, 21
Manasseh, Leonard
    architectural education 3
    early practice 8–16
    family background 1
    forms partnership with Ian Baker 16, 21
    images of *2*, *4*, *5*, *7*, *8*, *86*, *121*, *131*, *133*
    marriage 9, 22
    military service 4–5, *7*
    paintings and drawings *6*, *22*, *42*, *120*, 131,
        132
    as president of the AA 7–8
    professional outlook 21, 41–3, 46, 135–6
    public roles 119, 121
    retirement 130, *133*
    student work *4*, *5*
    teaching work *4*, *5*
    see also Leonard Manasseh Partnership;
        Manasseh and Baker
Manasseh, Philip and Renée, private house
        23–4
Manasseh, Phineas 20, *116*, 117
Manasseh, Sarah (second wife of Leonard) 22
Manasseh, Sylvia (sister of Leonard) 1, 2, 3, 9,
        10, 21, *131*
Manasseh, Zac 101
Manasseh and Baker 18, 21, 79
    Bath office 77, *78*
    change of name 125
    design language 79
    Rathbone Street office 72–4, *73*
    see also under the names of specific projects
Marland, Michael 49
Martin, Leslie 15, 53
Master Builder's House Hotel *110*, 111

McGuire, Penny 123
Medd, David 8
Meyer, Donald 79
Ministry of Defence housing 61, 130, 143, 152–3
Modular Concrete Company Ltd 55
Moggridge, Hal 90, 93, 94
Montagu of Beaulieu, Edward Douglas-Scott-
        Montagu 96–7
Morgan, Roger W. 72
Moro, Peter 73
motorway service station 44, *46*
Moya, Hidalgo 10, 15
'Museum of the Year' award 109

National Heritage award 109
National Motor Museum 96–111, *102*, *103*, *107*,
        108, *109*
    Brabazon restaurant 104, *105*, *106*, *134*
    model *86*, *100*
    plans *98*, *101*
    revised scheme 128
National Trust 119, 121
National Westminster Bank, Finchley 76
New Cavendish Pavilion (unbuilt) 128, *129*, 152
New Town housing 61–8
Newton Abbott, Forde House *118*, 126–7, 151
Niblet Hall, Inner Temple 150, *150*
Niemeyer, Oscar 47
North Westminster Community School 49

Ove Arup 71
Oxford, Magdalen College 92, 149

Palace Green 130, 153
partnerships *see* Leonard Manasseh
        Partnership; Manasseh and Baker
Partridge, John 77, 119
Partridge, Richard 77
Patrick Lynch Architects 72
Paziols, Perpignan, holiday home 33, 153
Pearce's Yard, Grantchester 34, *35*, 148
Perrett House sheltered housing 93, 150
Petersham, River Lane 30, 145
Pimlico, Lillington Gardens Estate 69
Port Lympne Wild Animal Park 149, *149*
Powell, Philip 3, 10, 15, 20
Press, Christopher *74*, 77, 125, 128, 130, 131
private houses 23–34, 39–40

public housing 34, 61–72, 77
Pulborough, private house 23

Queen's Parade, Bath, house 40, 149

Radipole Lake Pumping Station 84, *84*, 150
RAF housing 61, 130, 143, 152
Rathbone Street office 72–4, *73*, 130
Rea, Peter and Roseann, private house *28–9,*
    29–30, 144
Redcross Street, Bristol 77, 150
Regent's Park Boat House Café 131, 153
religious buildings 74
restaurant buildings 43–4, 104
RIBA (Royal Institute of British Architects)
    109, 119
River Lane, Petersham 30, 145
Riverside Close, Bridge, terraced houses 34,
    146
Roberts, John 68, 73
Robinson, Kenneth 97, 104–5
Roehampton, Bank Lane 28–9, *29–30*, 144
Rosenauer, Michael 16
Rosoman, Leonard *121*
Ross, Stuart 130, 131
Rotork works 37–9, *38*, *39*, 143
Rowntree, Diana 42, 48
Royal Academy 121–2
    Shop 122, *122*, 151
    Summer Exhibition 77, 122
Royal Air Force housing 61, 130, 143
Royal Fine Art Commission (RFAC) 119, 125
Royal Institute of British Architects (RIBA)
    109, 119
Royal Lancaster Hotel 44, *45*
Royal Mews Museum, Windsor 75–6, *76*, 149
Royal Society of Arts scheme 122, *122*
Royal West of England Academy 121, *121*
Rutherford School 46–9, *47*, *48*, *49*, 142–3

Sandwich Bay, private house 32, *33*, 77
Scandinavian influences 5, 9, 15, 24, 61, 136
Scarsbrook, Geoffrey 44, 73, *74*, 75, 122, 125
school buildings 46–9, 77
Scott, Christopher 113
Seven Sisters Country Park 111
Shrewsbury Gospel Hall, Harlesden *75*, 147
Singapore office 21, 141

Singer family, private house 29
Smerrin, Eldridge 24
Smith, Susan Babington 3
Smithson, Peter and Alison 5, *20*, 135
Snowdon scheme 93, *93*
South Grove, Highgate, private house 24–5,
    25, 142
Speight, Sadie 15
Spence, Basil 15, 99
Stamford Hall 61
Steeplehall Estate, Basildon 66–8, *66*, *67*, 145
Stevenage New Town Corporation 9
Strutt & Parker 96, 98
Stutchbury, Howard 80
Sutton, James 94, 109, 115

Teignbridge District Council 126–7
Teignmouth terminal (unbuilt) 125, *126–7*, 151
Thake, John 73
Theale Depot 95–6, *95*, 148
Time and Life office building 16, 140–1
Torr Quarry 94, *94*, 149
Trinidad courthouse (unbuilt) 150
Turkey, offices and laboratories 43, 143

University of Leicester 58–61, 144, 145

Ventris, Michael 24
Victoria and Albert Museum 'Space Rig'
    (unbuilt) 122–3, *123*, 150

Waterloo, Dodson Street Estate 32, 68–70, *69*,
    144
Waterloo Road housing 69–70, 150
Wayne Kerr headquarters 43, *43*, 141, 145
Wellington Country Park 113–17, *114*, *115*, 148
Wessex Water project 83–4
Williger, Karin *see* Manasseh, Karin (first wife
    of Leonard)
Windsor Royal Mews Museum 75–6, *76*, 149
Wornum, Grey 18
Worskett, Roy 81
Wright, John, private house 23
Wright, Lance 110, 111, 115

Yeoman (Morvern) Ltd 96

Zenghelis, Elia 136

Picture Credits

The author and publisher have made every effort to contact copyright holders and will be happy to correct, in subsequent editions, any errors or omissions that are brought to their attention.